Collins Junior Atlas

Editorial advisor Dr. Stephen Scoffham

Contents

Published by Collins
An imprint of HarperCollins Publishers
Westerhill Road
Bishopbriggs
Glasgow G64 2QT
www.harpercollins.co.uk

Fourth edition 2017

© HarperCollins Publishers 2017
Maps © Collins Bartholomew Ltd 2017

Collins ® is a registered trademark of HarperCollins Publishers Ltd

ISBN 978-0-00-820309-2

10 9 8 7 6 5 4 3

IN ASSOCIATION WITH

Geographical Association

MIX
Paper from responsible sources
FSC
www.fsc.org
FSC™ C007454

This book is produced from independently certified FSC™ paper to ensure responsible forest management.

For more information visit: www.harpercollins.co.uk/green

Printed by PNB Print, Latvia

All mapping in this atlas is generated from Collins Bartholomew digital databases. Collins Bartholomew, the UK's leading independent geographical information supplier, can provide a digital, custom, and premium mapping service to a variety of markets.
For further information:
Tel: +44 (0) 208 307 4515
e-mail: collinsbartholomew@harpercollins.co.uk
or visit our website at: www.collinsbartholomew.com

If you would like to comment on any aspect of this book, please contact us at the above address or online.

www.collins.co.uk
e-mail: collinsmaps@harpercollins.co.uk

Globes

Globes are models of the Earth. They show the true shape and size of the continents.

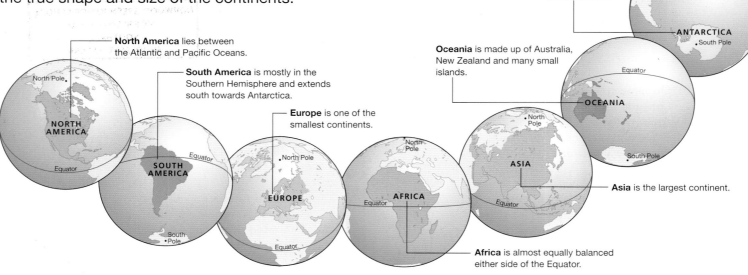

North America lies between the Atlantic and Pacific Oceans.

South America is mostly in the Southern Hemisphere and extends south towards Antarctica.

Europe is one of the smallest continents.

Oceania is made up of Australia, New Zealand and many small islands.

Antarctica encircles the South Pole.

Asia is the largest continent.

Africa is almost equally balanced either side of the Equator.

Map projections

To show the world on a flat map we need to peel the surface of the globe and flatten it out. There are many different methods of drawing atlas maps. These methods are called **projections.**

Every map projection shows the continents a different shape and size. The projection used for world maps in this atlas is called Eckert IV.

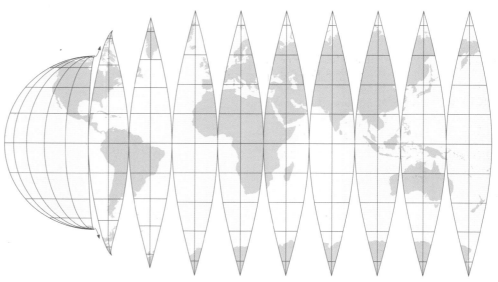

This is how the Earth would look if the surface could be peeled and laid flat.

Which way up?

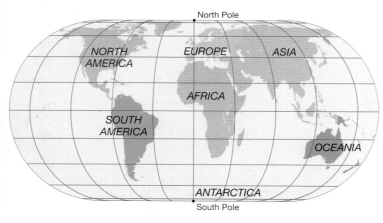

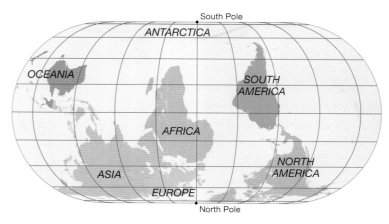

World maps are usually drawn with the North Pole at the top. Can you find Europe?

This map is just as accurate but has the South Pole at the top. Where is Europe now?

Latitude and longitude

We use latitude and longitude to locate places on the Earth's surface. Lines of **latitude** are imaginary lines. They are numbered in degrees North or South of the Equator.

Lines of **longitude** are imaginary lines which run from the North to the South Poles. They are numbered in degrees East or West of a line through London known as the Greenwich Meridian.

Lines of latitude

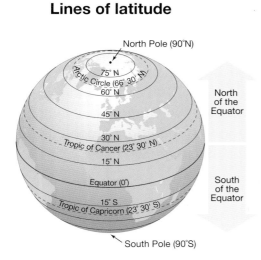

Lines of longitude

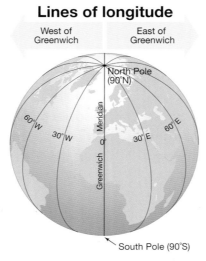

Lines of latitude and longitude

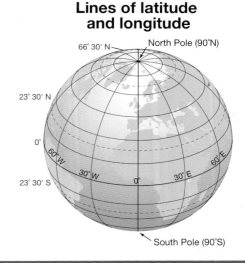

Hemispheres

The Equator divides the globe into two halves. All land north of the Equator is called the Northern Hemisphere. Land south of the Equator is called the Southern Hemisphere. 0° and 180° lines of longitude also divide the globes into two imaginary halves, the Western and Eastern Hemispheres.

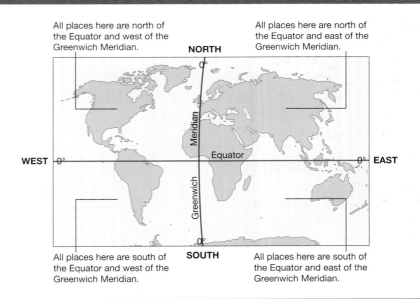

All places here are north of the Equator and west of the Greenwich Meridian.

All places here are north of the Equator and east of the Greenwich Meridian.

All places here are south of the Equator and west of the Greenwich Meridian.

All places here are south of the Equator and east of the Greenwich Meridian.

Grid references

As well as using lines of latitude to find places, this atlas uses grids. The columns are labelled with a letter and the rows with a number. The grid code e.g. D4 can be used to find all places within one grid square.

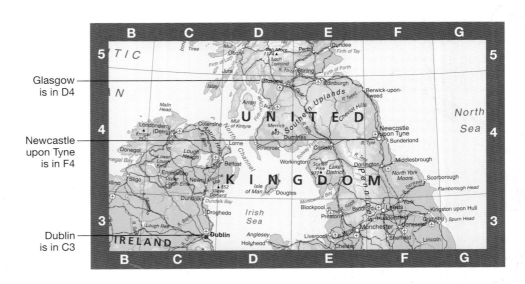

Glasgow is in D4

Newcastle upon Tyne is in F4

Dublin is in C3

What is an atlas?

An atlas is a book of maps. The maps in the first part of this atlas tell you about the United Kingdom. The next maps tell you about the continents, while those near the end show the whole world. Some of the maps focus on themes or topics. There is an index at the back to help you find where places are.

Most of the maps in this atlas are about people and their surroundings. For example, you can find out where people live, how they travel from place to place and about the plants and scenery in different parts of the world. Photographs, charts and diagrams provide extra information. There are files with lots of interesting facts.

Atlas makers have to make many choices. They have to decide which places to include and which places to leave out. It's impossible to show everything. They also try to choose things which you will find interesting. Each page is full of information.

Our world never stays the same. This atlas tells you about the world today. The choices that people make will change the world in the years to come. Thinking about the future reminds us that the Earth is the only home we have.

Understanding maps

Special names and numbers are used to label parts of an atlas map.

Page number
This helps you to find out where the map you want is in the atlas.

Locator map
This shows the part of the world covered by the map.

Page introduction
These contain interesting information about a country.

Latitude and longitude
These blue lines indicate distance north or south of the Equator and east or west of the Greenwich Meridian.

Scale
This explains how large a map is. It helps to work out distances between places. See page 5 to find out more about scale.

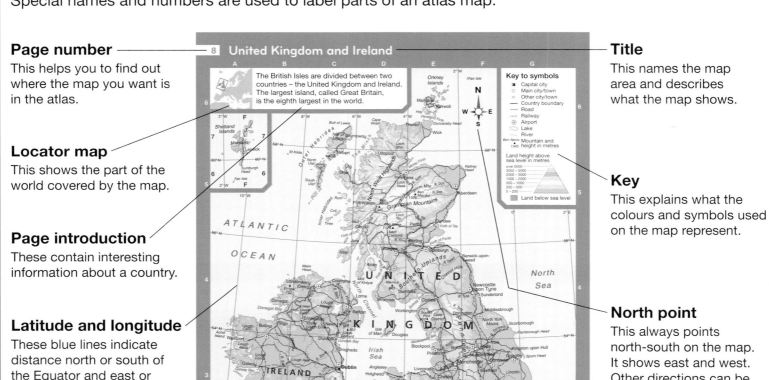

Title
This names the map area and describes what the map shows.

Key
This explains what the colours and symbols used on the map represent.

North point
This always points north-south on the map. It shows east and west. Other directions can be found from the north point.

Grid references
The numbers and letters along the edges of the map help to locate the places listed in the atlas index.

Scale

Maps are much smaller than the regions they show. To compare the real area with the mapped area you have to use a scale. Each map in this atlas shows its scale. This is shown using a scale bar which is explained in words.

E.g.

| 0 | 200 | 400 | 600 | 800 km |

Scale : One centimetre on this map is the same as 200 kilometres on the ground.

Measuring distance

The scale bar can be used to measure how far it is between places.

For example, the straight line distance between London and Birmingham on the map below is 4 centimetres.

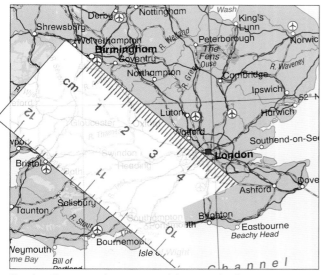

Scale: One centimetre on this map is the same as 40 kilometres on the ground.

| 0 | 40 | 80 | 120 | 160 km |

Look at the ruler.
One centimetre on this map is the same as 40 kilometres on the ground.
The real distance between London and Birmingham is therefore 160 kilometres (i.e. 4 x 40).

Small scale

Scale: One centimetre on this map is the same as 800 kilometres on the ground.

| 0 | 800 | 1600 | 2400 | 3200 km |

Medium scale

Scale: One centimetre on this map is the same as 250 kilometres on the ground.

| 0 | 250 | 500 | 750 | 1000 | 1250 km |

Large scale

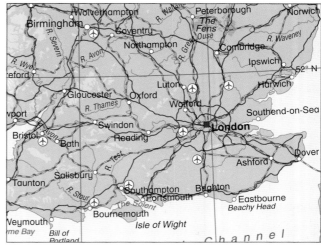

Scale: One centimetre on this map is the same as 40 kilometres on the ground.

| 0 | 40 | 80 | 120 | 160 | 200 km |

Small scale maps show larger areas with less detail.

Large scale maps show smaller areas with more detail.

Finding directions

Directions help you to work out which way to go when you travel from place to place. There are four main compass directions: North (N), East (E), South (S) and West (W). These are called the cardinal points. The compass can also be divided in eight or sixteen points as shown in the diagram below.

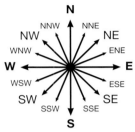

A sixteen-point compass

The needle of the compass always points to the north because it is magnetic. Maps are usually drawn to match the compass with north at the top and south at the bottom.

Moon and tides

Tides are caused by the gravitational pull of the Sun and the Moon. When the Sun and Moon are lined up they pull together causing strong (spring) tides which rise very high and drop very low. When the Sun and Moon pull in different directions it causes much weaker (neap) tides.

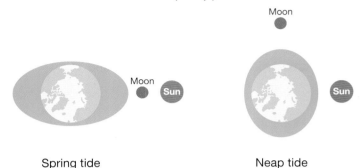

Spring tide   Neap tide

The Moon takes 29 days to orbit the Earth. This means that spring and neap tides occur approximately once a month. The Sun and Moon also travel through the sky each day as the Earth rotates. This creates two high tides a day.

Time zones

Time varies around the world as the Earth spins. This causes different parts of the world to be in light or dark at any single moment.

Time zones have been created so that the Sun peaks around midday all over the world. Clocks need to be changed by an hour for every 15 degrees of longitude of travel.

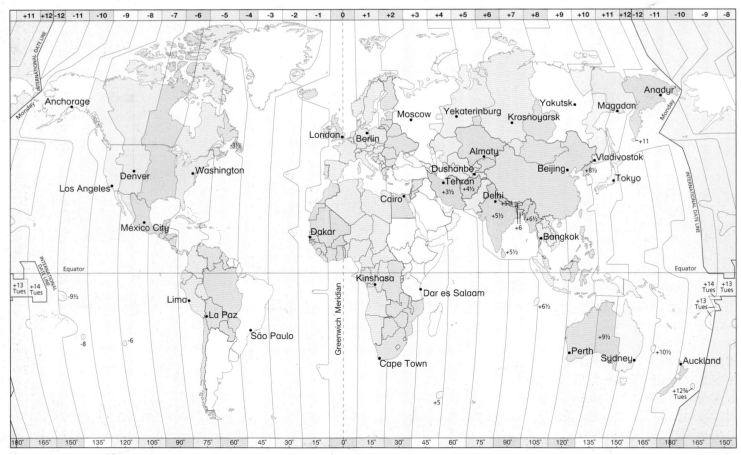

The seasons

The Earth's axis is tilted by 23½ degrees in relation to the Sun. As a result places are either tilted away or towards the Sun at different times of year. In the UK this results in four different seasons – spring, summer, autumn and winter.

March 21 (spring equinox)
The Sun is overhead at the Equator and all places have equal day and night. This is known as the spring equinox. Places in the Northern Hemisphere have three months of spring. Places in the Southern Hemisphere have three months of autumn.

June 21 (summer solstice)
The Sun is now overhead at the Tropic of Cancer (23½ degrees north). This is known as the summer solstice. Inside the Arctic Circle (66½ degrees north) the Sun never sets.

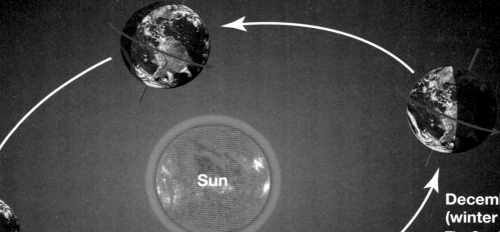

December 21 (winter solstice)
The Sun is now overhead at the Tropic of Capricorn (23½ degrees south). This is known as the winter solstice. Inside the Arctic Circle (66½ degrees north) there is continual darkness.

September 21 (autumn equinox)
The Sun is overhead at the Equator and all places have equal day and night. This is known as the autumn equinox. Places in the Northern Hemisphere have three months of autumn. Places in the Southern Hemisphere have three months of spring.

Day and night

It takes the Earth 24 hours to rotate on its axis. At any one moment half the Earth is facing the Sun and in sunlight. The other half is facing away from the Sun and in darkness.

The rotation of the Earth causes the cycle of day and night. It also creates the apparent movement of the Sun from east to west across the sky.

Direction of rotation

Cycle of day and night in the UK at the spring and autumn equinox

Dawn in the UK

Midday in the UK

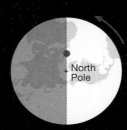

Dusk in the UK

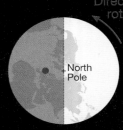

Midnight in the UK

The British Isles are divided between two countries – the United Kingdom and Ireland. The largest island, called Great Britain, is the eighth largest in the world.

Key to symbols

- ■ Capital city
- ○ Main city/town
- ○ Other city/town
- — Country boundary
- — Road
- -- Railway
- ✈ Airport
- ～ Lake
- ～ River
- ▲ Ben Nevis 1345 Mountain and height in metres

Land height above sea level in metres

- over 5000
- 3000 – 5000
- 2000 – 3000
- 1000 – 2000
- 500 – 1000
- 200 – 500
- 0 – 200

Land below sea level

N W E S

Shetland Islands
Mainland, Lerwick, Sumburgh Head, Fair Isle

Orkney Islands
Mainland, Kirkwall, Hoy, Pentland Firth

ATLANTIC OCEAN

Fair Isle, Cape Wrath, Thurso, Duncansby Head, Wick

Butt of Lewis, Isle of Lewis, Stornoway, Loch Shin, Ullapool, Moray Firth, Rattray Head

Outer Hebrides, The Minch, St Kilda, Tarbert, Harris, North Uist, Uig, Skye, South Uist, Rum, Coll, Tiree, Mull, Oban, Jura, Islay, Arran

Inner Hebrides

North West Highlands, Inverness, Loch Ness, R. Spey, Cairngorm Mts, Ben Macdui 1309, R. Don, R. Dee, Aberdeen

Ben Nevis 1345, Fort William, Grampian Mountains, Ben More 1174, Loch Tay, R. Tay, Perth, Dundee, Firth of Tay, Loch Lomond, R. Forth, Stirling, Firth of Forth

Glasgow, Edinburgh, Berwick-upon-Tweed, R. Tweed, Cheviot Hills

UNITED KINGDOM

Malin Head, Londonderry (Derry), Errigal 752, Coleraine, Antrim Hills, R. Foyle, R. Bann, Larne, Donegal, Lower Lough Erne, Lough Neagh, R. Lagan, Belfast, Donegal Bay, Enniskillen, Upper Lough Erne, Newry, Sligo, Mourne Mts, Slieve Donard 852, Dundalk, Dundalk Bay

North Channel, Mull of Kintyre, Ayr, Merrick 843, Southern Uplands, Dumfries, R. Nith, Stranraer, Solway Firth, Carlisle, Workington, R. Tyne, Newcastle upon Tyne, Sunderland, Middlesbrough, Darlington, R. Tees, Scafell Pike 977, Lake District, North York Moors, Scarborough, R. Derwent, Flamborough Head

Pennines

Ballina, Lough Conn, Westport, Achill Island, Lough Mask, Lough Corrib, Galway, Galway Bay

IRELAND

R. Moy, R. Shannon, Lough Ree, R. Boyle, Lough Derg, R. Suck, R. Shannon, Limerick, Tralee, R. Nore, R. Barrow, Carrauntoohil 1041, R. Lee, Cork, Cape Clear

R. Liffey, Dublin, Drogheda, Wicklow Mts, Wicklow, Wicklow Head, Wexford, Rosslare, Waterford, R. Suir, R. Blackwater

Irish Sea

Isle of Man, Douglas, Morecambe Bay, Blackpool, Preston, R. Ribble, Bradford, Leeds, York, Kingston upon Hull, Spurn Head, Grimsby, Huddersfield, Doncaster, Lincoln, Manchester, Liverpool, R. Mersey, Sheffield, Chester, Crewe, Stoke-on-Trent, Nottingham, R. Trent, Derby, Shrewsbury, Wolverhampton, Birmingham, Coventry, Northampton, Peterborough, The Fens, Norwich, R. Waveney, King's Lynn, The Wash, R. Welland, R. Great Ouse, Cambridge, Ipswich

Anglesey, Holyhead, Caernarfon, Snowdon 1085, R. Dee, Cambrian Mountains, Cardigan Bay, Aberystwyth, R. Severn, R. Wye, Hereford, Brecon Beacons 886, Pembroke, Fishguard, St David's Head, Swansea, Cardiff, Newport, Gloucester, R. Thames, Oxford, Luton, Watford, Harwich, Southend-on-Sea, London, Reading, Swindon, Bath, R. Avon, Bristol, Bristol Channel

St George's Channel, Celtic Sea

Exmoor, Taunton, Salisbury, R. Stour, Southampton, Portsmouth, Brighton, Eastbourne, Beachy Head, The Solent, Isle of Wight, Bournemouth, Weymouth, Lyme Bay, Bill of Portland, Dover, Ashford

Bodmin Moor, Dartmoor 619, R. Exe, R. Teign, Exeter, Plymouth, Penzance, Land's End, Isles of Scilly, Lizard Point

English Channel, FRANCE, Dieppe

North Sea

Scale : One centimetre on this map is the same as 40 kilometres on the ground

0 50 100 150 200 250 300 km

Four countries make up the United Kingdom or UK. They are England, Scotland, Wales and Northern Ireland. The Isle of Man and Channel Islands are not part of the UK and have their own laws.

Key to symbols

 Countries
■ Capital city
● National capital
○ Important city/town

Shetland Islands

Orkney Islands

ATLANTIC OCEAN

Outer Hebrides

Inverness

Aberdeen

Fort William

SCOTLAND

Dundee

North Sea

Glasgow

Edinburgh

Londonderry (Derry)

NORTHERN IRELAND

Belfast

Newcastle upon Tyne

Middlesbrough

UNITED KINGDOM

IRELAND

Isle of Man

Irish Sea

Blackpool

Preston

York

Bradford

Leeds

Dublin ■

Manchester

Liverpool

Sheffield

Stoke-on-Trent

Derby

Nottingham

ENGLAND

Norwich

Wolverhampton

Leicester

Birmingham

Coventry

Cambridge

WALES

Ipswich

Swansea

Oxford

London ■

Southend-on-Sea

Cardiff

Bristol

Reading

BELGIUM

Southampton

Brighton

Portsmouth

Bournemouth

Plymouth

Torquay

English Channel

Channel Islands

FRANCE

The UK government makes laws in the Houses of Parliament in London.

0 50 100 150 200 250 300 km

Scale : One centimetre on this map is the same as 50 kilometres on the ground.

Key to symbols

International boundary
National boundary
Administrative boundary

The four countries of the United Kingdom are divided into counties and administrative areas. The smallest areas are in towns and cities where people live close together. The largest areas such as Highland, North Yorkshire, Cumbria and Powys include remote moors and mountains.

N
W E
S

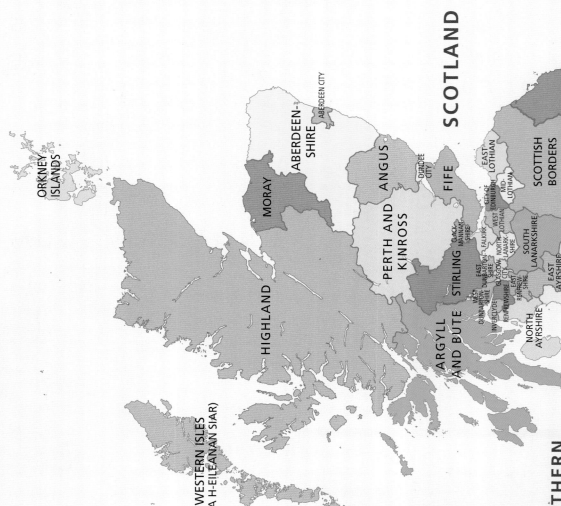

SHETLAND ISLANDS

ORKNEY ISLANDS

WESTERN ISLES
(NA H-EILEANAN SIAR)

HIGHLAND

MORAY

ABERDEEN-SHIRE

ABERDEEN CITY

SCOTLAND

ANGUS

DUNDEE CITY

PERTH AND KINROSS

FIFE

EAST LOTHIAN

CITY OF EDINBURGH

MID-LOTHIAN

WEST LOTHIAN

FALKIRK

CLACK-MANNAN-SHIRE

STIRLING

ARGYLL AND BUTE

WEST DUNBARTON-SHIRE

EAST DUNBARTON-SHIRE

GLASGOW CITY

NORTH LANARK-SHIRE

EAST RENFREW-SHIRE

INVERCLYDE

RENFREWSHIRE

SOUTH LANARKSHIRE

NORTH AYRSHIRE

EAST AYRSHIRE

SOUTH AYRSHIRE

SCOTTISH BORDERS

NORTHUMBERLAND

NEWCASTLE UPON

NORTH TYNESIDE

DUMFRIES AND GALLOWAY

NORTHERN IRELAND

CAUSEWAY COAST AND GLENS

0   30   60   90   120   150 km

Scale : One centimetre on this map is the same as 30 kilometres on the ground.

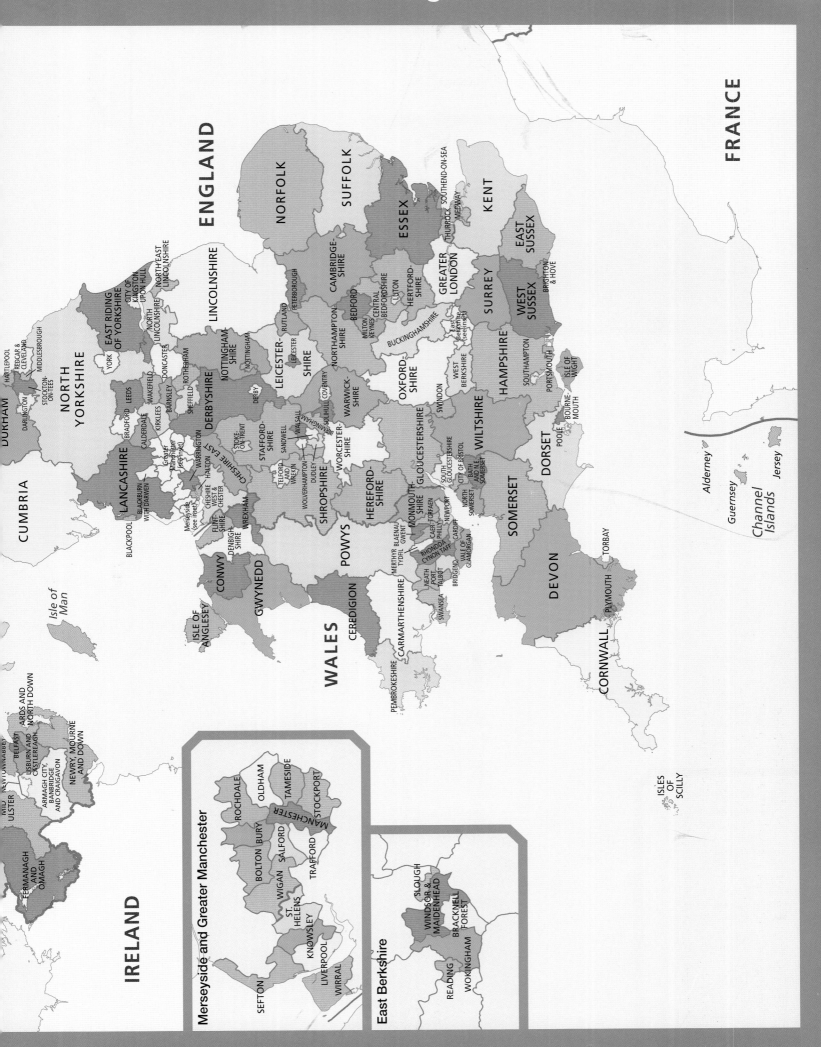

FRANCE

ENGLAND

NORFOLK

SUFFOLK

ESSEX

KENT

EAST SUSSEX

SURREY

WEST SUSSEX

GREATER LONDON

SOUTHEND-ON-SEA

THURROCK

MEDWAY

HAMPSHIRE

SOUTHAMPTON

PORTSMOUTH

ISLE OF WIGHT

BOURNE-MOUTH

POOLE

DORSET

WILTSHIRE

DEVON

SOMERSET

CORNWALL

PLYMOUTH

TORBAY

ISLES OF SCILLY

Alderney

Guernsey

Jersey

Channel Islands

DURHAM

HARTLEPOOL

REDCAR & CLEVELAND

MIDDLESBROUGH

STOCKTON-ON-TEES

DARLINGTON

NORTH YORKSHIRE

YORK

EAST RIDING OF YORKSHIRE

CITY OF KINGSTON UPON HULL

NORTH-EAST LINCOLNSHIRE

NORTH LINCOLNSHIRE

LINCOLNSHIRE

CAMBRIDGE-SHIRE

PETERBOROUGH

RUTLAND

LEICESTER-SHIRE

LEICESTER

NOTTINGHAM-SHIRE

NOTTINGHAM

DERBYSHIRE

DERBY

BRADFORD

LEEDS

CALDERDALE

WAKEFIELD

KIRKLEES

BARNSLEY

DONCASTER

ROTHERHAM

SHEFFIELD

NORTHAMPTON-SHIRE

BEDFORD

CENTRAL BEDFORDSHIRE

LUTON

MILTON KEYNES

HERTFORD-SHIRE

BUCKINGHAMSHIRE

OXFORD-SHIRE

SWINDON

WEST BERKSHIRE

East Berkshire (see inset)

WARWICK-SHIRE

COVENTRY

SOLIHULL

BIRMINGHAM

WALSALL

SANDWELL

DUDLEY

WOLVERHAMPTON

WORCESTER-SHIRE

GLOUCESTERSHIRE

HEREFORD-SHIRE

STAFFORD-SHIRE

STOKE-ON-TRENT

TELFORD AND WREKIN

SHROPSHIRE

CHESHIRE EAST

CHESHIRE WEST & CHESTER

WARRINGTON

HALTON

Greater Manchester (see inset)

Merseyside (see inset)

LANCASHIRE

BLACKBURN WITH DARWEN

BLACKPOOL

CUMBRIA

Isle of Man

WREXHAM

FLINT-SHIRE

DENBIGH-SHIRE

CONWY

GWYNEDD

ISLE OF ANGLESEY

POWYS

CEREDIGION

WALES

CARMARTHENSHIRE

PEMBROKESHIRE

MONMOUTH-SHIRE

TORFAEN

NEWPORT

CAER-PHILLY

BLAENAU GWENT

MERTHYR TYDFIL

RHONDDA CYNON TAFF

CARDIFF

VALE OF GLAMORGAN

BRIDGEND

NEATH PORT TALBOT

SWANSEA

SOUTH GLOUCESTERSHIRE

CITY OF BRISTOL

BATH AND N.E. SOMERSET

NORTH SOMERSET

IRELAND

NEWTOWNABBEY

BELFAST

ARDS AND NORTH DOWN

LISBURN AND CASTLEREAGH

ARMAGH CITY, BANBRIDGE AND CRAIGAVON

NEWRY, MOURNE AND DOWN

MID ULSTER

FERMANAGH AND OMAGH

Merseyside and Greater Manchester

ROCHDALE

OLDHAM

TAMESIDE

STOCKPORT

MANCHESTER

BURY

BOLTON

WIGAN

SALFORD

TRAFFORD

ST. HELENS

KNOWSLEY

SEFTON

LIVERPOOL

WIRRAL

East Berkshire

SLOUGH

WINDSOR & MAIDENHEAD

BRACKNELL FOREST

READING

WOKINGHAM

The Scottish highlands are the emptiest part of the UK. There are many small islands around the coast. They are linked to the mainland by ferry.

Scotland has many mountains. Those which are over 3000 feet (914 m) high are called Munros. This one is in Glen Coe near Ben Nevis.

ATLANTIC OCEAN

Flannan Isles

St Kilda

Outer Hebrides

Butt of Lewis
Port of Ness
Tolsta Head
Great Bernera
Stornoway
Lewis
Port Nan Giùran
Eye Peninsula
Loch Langavat
Scarp
Kebock Head
Clishham 799
Tarbert
Scalpay
Harris
Rubha Reidh
Pabbay
Berneray
Rodel
Sound of Harris
Rubha Hunish
North Uist
Lochmaddy
Loch Snizort
Uig
Rona
Monach Islands
Benbecula
Dunvegan
The Storr 719
Portree
Raasay
South Uist
Skye
Beinn Mhor 620
Scalpay
Kyle of Lochalsh
Kyleakin
Lochboisdale
Cuillin Hills 993 928
Sgurr Alasdair Blaven
Soay
Cuillin Sound
Canna
Ardvasar
Sound of Barra
Eriskay
Rum
Askival
Barra
Sheabhal 383
Vatersay Castlebay
Mallaig
Sandray
Eigg
Loch Morar
Mingulay
Muck
Sound of Arisaig
Inner Hebrides
Point of Ardnamurchan
Coll
Ben Hogh 104
Arinagour
Tobermory
Tiree
Scarinish

Cape Wrath
Durness
Kinlochbervie
Handa Island
Foinaven 915
Scourie
Loch More
Point of Stoer
Lochinver
Loch Assynt
Ben More Assynt 998
Summer Isles
The Minch
Ullapool
Loch Broom
An Teallach 1062
Fionn Loch
Gairloch
Loch Ewe
Loch Maree
Sgurr Mor 1110
WESTER ROSS
R. Orrin
Sgurr a'Choire Gh 1083
Loch Monar
Carn Eighe 1183
Glen Affric
R. Moriston
Inner Sound
L. Torridon
North West
Sound of Sleat
Loch Hourn
Loch Cluanie
R. Garry
Glen Shiel
Ladhar Bheinn 1020
Loch Quoich
Glen Garry
Loch Arkaig
Loch Lochy
Gulvain 983
Loch Shiel
Sgurr Dhomhnuill 888
Fort William
Ben Nevis 1345
Loch Leven
Glen Coe
Bidean nam Bian 1150
Kinlochle
Morvern
Loch Sunart
Loch Linnhe
Loch Frisa
Lochaline
Sound of Mull
Loch Etive
Augusti
Loch
Fo

Key to symbols

○ Main city/town
○ Other city/town
— Road
▭ Railway
✈ Airport
▱ Lake
～ River
▲ Ben Nevis / 1345 Mountain and height in metres

Land height above sea level in metres

over 1500
1000 – 1500
900 – 1000
500 – 900
200 – 500
100 – 200
0 – 100

Main Map

4° W 3° W 2° W

Fair Isle

Papa Westray
Westray
North Ronaldsay
N. Ronaldsay Firth
Eday
Rousay
Sanday
Brough Head
Orkney Islands
Loch of Harray
Stronsay
Stronsay Firth
Shapinsay
Mainland
Kirkwall
Stromness
Skaill
59° N
Ward Hill 479
Scapa Flow
Flotta
Hoy
Burray
South Ronaldsay
Burwick
Pentland Firth
Dunnet Head
John o'Groats
Thurso B.
Duncansby Head
Dounreay
Thurso
Bettyhill
Loch Watten
Sinclair's Bay
Tongue
Loch Loyal
R. Wick
Wick
CAITHNESS
R. Thurso
SUTHERLAND
961 Ben Klibreck
Loch Rimsdale
Lybster
R. Helmsdale
Helmsdale
Lairg
R. Brora
N O R T H
Brora
Golspie
S E A
Dornoch Firth
Tarbat Ness
Tain
Moray Firth
Invergordon
58° N
Cromarty Firth
Lossiemouth
Cullen
Fraserburgh
Ben Wyvis
Black Isle
Kinloss
Buckie
Macduff
Dingwall
Fortrose
Elgin
Banff
Rattray Head
Conon Bridge
Nairn
Forres
Fochabers
R. Deveron
Crimond
Moray Firth
Rothes
Knock Hill 430
Turriff
Mintlaw
Beauly
Inverness
R. Ness
R. Nairn
Keith
R. Isla
Peterhead
R. Findhorn
Dufftown
Huntly
R. Ythan
Strathspey
STRATHBOGIE
Cruden Bay
Grantown-on-Spey
R. Bogie
Oldmeldrum
Ellon
SCOTLAND
R. Don
Inverurie
Monadhliath Mountains
Aviemore
Kintore
Dyce
Cairn Gorm 1245
R. Avon
Aberdeen
Kingussie
Cairngorm Mts
Newtonmore
Ben Macdui 1309
Aboyne
R. Dee
Banchory
Laggan
Braemar
Ballater
57° N
R. Spey
Carn nan Gabhar 1121
R. Dee
Dalwhinnie
1155
Stonehaven
Ben Alder
Lochnagar
Glenshee
North R. Esk
Inverbervie
Grampian Mountains
Blair Atholl
Backwater Reservoir
Laurencekirk
L. Rannoch
1083 Schiehallion
Loch Tummel
Pitlochry
R. Isla
Brechin
Rannoch Moor
R. Tummel
Kirriemuir
Montrose
Ben Lawers 1214
R. Lyon
Aberfeldy
Blairgowrie
Forfar
4° W
Coupar Angus
Sidlaw Hills
Strathmore
Arbroath
3° W
Carnoustie
2° W

Inset Map (Shetland Islands)

2° W 1° W

Herma Ness
Unst
Point of Fethaland
Yell Sound
Fetlar
Ronas Hill 450
Yell
Toft
Out Skerries
St. Magnus Bay
Muckle Roe
Whalsay
Papa Stour
Mainland
Foula
Shetland Islands
Lerwick
Bressay
60° N
Sumburgh
Sumburgh Head
Fair Isle

2° W 1° W

Platforms in the North Sea are used to bring oil ashore from rocks under the ocean.

Northern Ireland is the smallest country in the UK. Most places are less than 100 km from the capital, Belfast. Lough Neagh is a large lake in the middle of Northern Ireland.

After many years of fighting, Catholics and Protestants now work together to govern Northern Ireland from Stormont.

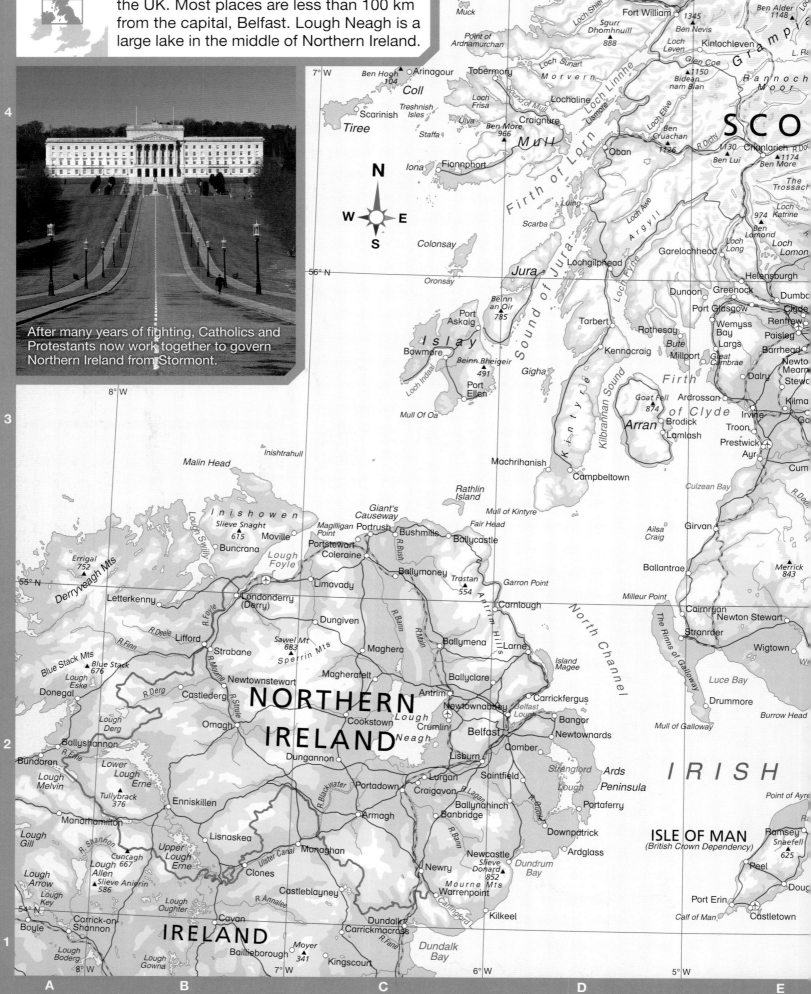

Scale : One centimetre on this map is the same as 12.5 kilometres on the ground.

0   25   50   75 km

Most people in Scotland live in the central lowlands. The biggest cities, Edinburgh and Glasgow, are less than 70 km apart.

Important routes lead north from Edinburgh across the Firth of Forth to other parts of Scotland.

Key to symbols

- Country capital
- Main city/town
- Other city/town
- Country boundary
- Road
- Railway
- ⊕ Airport
- Lake
- River
- Ben Nevis ▲ 1345 Mountain and height in metres

Land height above sea level in metres

- over 1500
- 1000 – 1500
- 900 – 1000
- 500 – 900
- 200 – 500
- 100 – 200
- 0 – 100

NORTH SEA

ENGLAND

SCOTLAND

The Pennine hills run southwards from Scotland through northern England. Old industrial cities such as Manchester, Bradford and Sheffield are found on the edge of the Pennines.

Tourists come to Derwent Water and other parts of the Lake District to enjoy the beautiful scenery.

Scale : One centimetre on this map is the same as 12.5 kilometres on the ground.

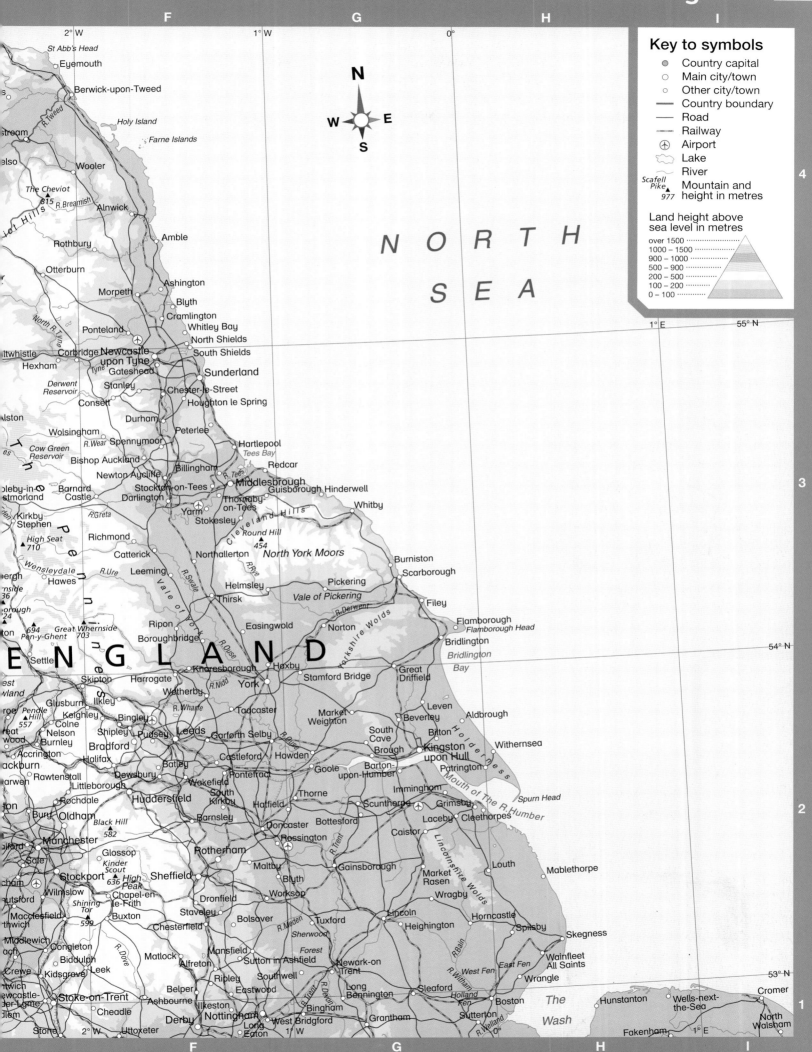

Key to symbols

- ● Country capital
- ◎ Main city/town
- ○ Other city/town
- ── Country boundary
- ── Road
- ┈ Railway
- ✈ Airport
- Lake
- River
- *Scafell Pike* ▲ Mountain and
  977 height in metres

Land height above
sea level in metres

- over 1500
- 1000 – 1500
- 900 – 1000
- 500 – 900
- 200 – 500
- 100 – 200
- 0 – 100

NORTH
SEA

St Abb's Head
Eyemouth
Berwick-upon-Tweed
R.Tweed
stream
Holy Island
Farne Islands
Kelso
Wooler
The Cheviot
815 R.Breamish
Alnwick
Cheviot Hills
Rothbury
Amble
Otterburn
Morpeth
Ashington
Blyth
Cramlington
North R.Tyne
Ponteland
Whitley Bay
ltwhistle
Corbridge Newcastle
upon Tyne
North Shields
South Shields
Hexham
Tyne
Gateshead
Sunderland
Derwent
Reservoir
Stanley
Chester-le-Street
Consett
Houghton le Spring
Alston
Durham
Wolsingham
Peterlee
R.Wear
Spennymoor
Cow Green
Reservoir
Bishop Auckland
Hartlepool
Tees Bay
leby-in-
stmorland
Barnard
Castle
Newton Aycliffe
Billingham
Redcar
R.Tees
Stockton-on-Tees
Middlesbrough
Guisborough Hinderwell
Darlington
Thornaby-
on-Tees
Kirkby
Stephen
R.Greta
Yarm
Stokesley
Whitby
High Seat
710
Richmond
Round Hill
454
Cleveland Hills
Wensleydale
Catterick
Northallerton
North York Moors
rnside
36
Leeming
R.Ure
R.Swale
Helmsley
Burniston
Scarborough
Hawes
R.Rye
Pickering
Vale of York
Thirsk
Vale of Pickering
Filey
borough
24
Ripon
Easingwold
R.Derwent
Great Whernside
703
Boroughbridge
Norton
Flamborough
Flamborough Head
Pen-y-Ghent
Yorkshire Wolds
Bridlington
ENGLAND
Settle
Knaresborough
Haxby
Bridlington
Bay
Skipton
Harrogate
R.Nidd
York
Stamford Bridge
Great
Driffield
est
wland
Glusburn
Wetherby
Leven
Pendle
Hill
557
Ilkley
Bingley
R.Wharfe
Tadcaster
Market
Weighton
Beverley
Aldbrough
roe
Keighley
Colne
Shipley
Garforth Selby
South
Cave
Bilton
Nelson
Pudsey
Leeds
Brough
Kingston
upon Hull
Withernsea
eat
wood
Burnley
Bradford
Castleford
Howden
Barton-
upon-Humber
Holderness
Accrington
Halifax
Batley
Goole
Patrington
ackburn
Rawtenstall
Dewsbury
Pontefract
Thorne
Immingham
Mouth of The R.Humber
Spurn Head
arwen
Littleborough
Wakefield
South
Kirkby
Thorne
Scunthorpe
Grimsby
ton
Rochdale
Huddersfield
Hatfield
Barton-
upon-Humber
Laceby
Cleethorpes
Bury
Oldham
Barnsley
Doncaster
Bottesford
Caistor
Manchester
Black Hill
582
Rossington
R.Trent
Louth
Mablethorpe
Sale
Glossop
Rotherham
Gainsborough
Market
Rasen
Lincolnshire Wolds
Stockport
Kinder
Scout
Maltby
Blyth
Wragby
cham
High
Peak
Sheffield
ton
Wilmslow
636
Worksop
Lincoln
Horncastle
utsford
Chapel-en-
le-Frith
Dronfield
Staveley
Heighington
Spilsby
Skegness
Macclesfield
Shining
Tor
599
Buxton
Bolsover
Tuxford
Wainfleet
All Saints
twich
Chesterfield
R.Meden
Sherwood
West Fen
East Fen
Wrangle
Middlewich
R.Dove
Mansfield
Forest
Newark-on-
Trent
R.Bain
ach
Congleton
Matlock
Alfreton
Sutton in Ashfield
Lincoln
Holland
Crewe
Biddulph
Leek
Ripley
Southwell
West Fen
Sleaford
Boston
The
Wash
Hunstanton
Wells-next-
the-Sea
Cromer
ntwich
Kidsgrove
Belper
Eastwood
R.Witham
R.Bain
wcastle-
Lyme
Ashbourne
Ilkeston
Bingham
Long
Bennington
Sutterton
R.Welland
North
Walsham
lem
Stoke-on-Trent
Cheadle
Derby
Nottingham
West Bridgford
Grantham
R.Nene
Fakenham
Stone
Uttoxeter
Long
Eaton

Wales is well-known for its mountains, hills and valleys. The main towns are in the south and on the coast.

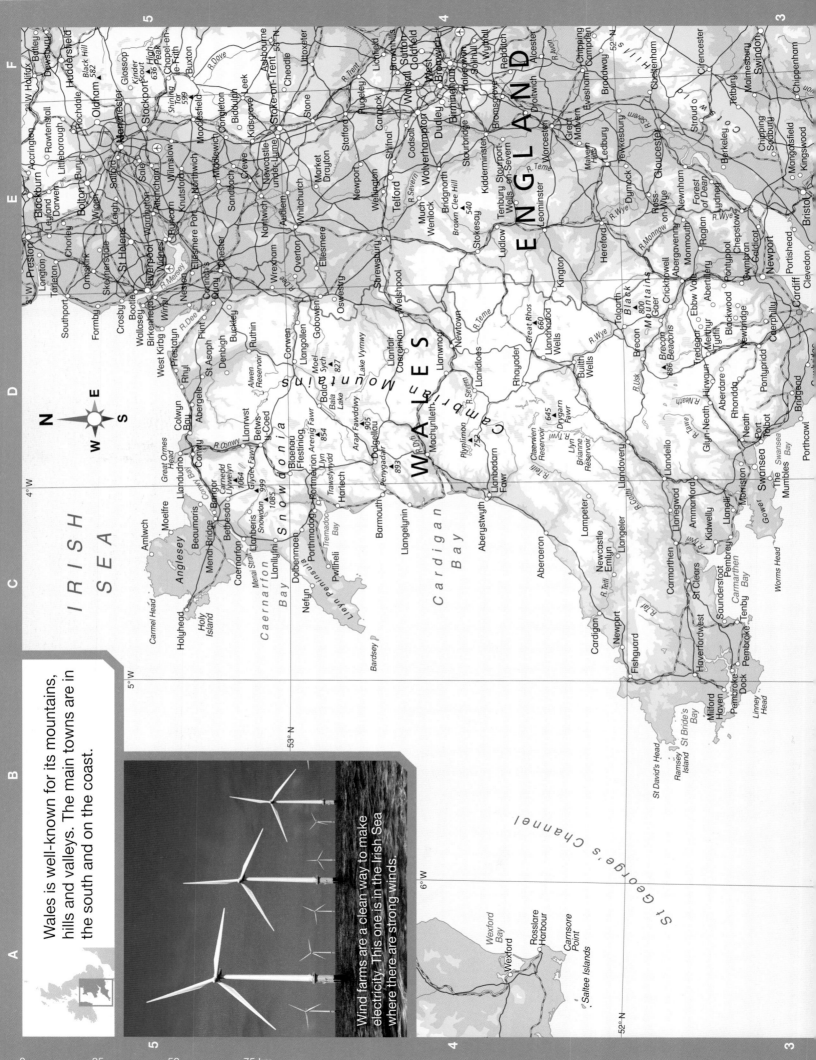

Wind farms are a clean way to make electricity. This one is in the Irish Sea where there are strong winds.

IRISH SEA

ENGLAND

WALES

Snowdonia

Cambrian Mountains

Berwyn Mountains

Black Mountains

Brecon Beacons

Anglesey

Holy Island

Llŷn Peninsula

Caernarfon Bay

Cardigan Bay

St George's Channel

N / E / S / W (compass)

Scale: One centimetre on this map is the same as 12.5 kilometres on the ground.

0   25   50   75 km

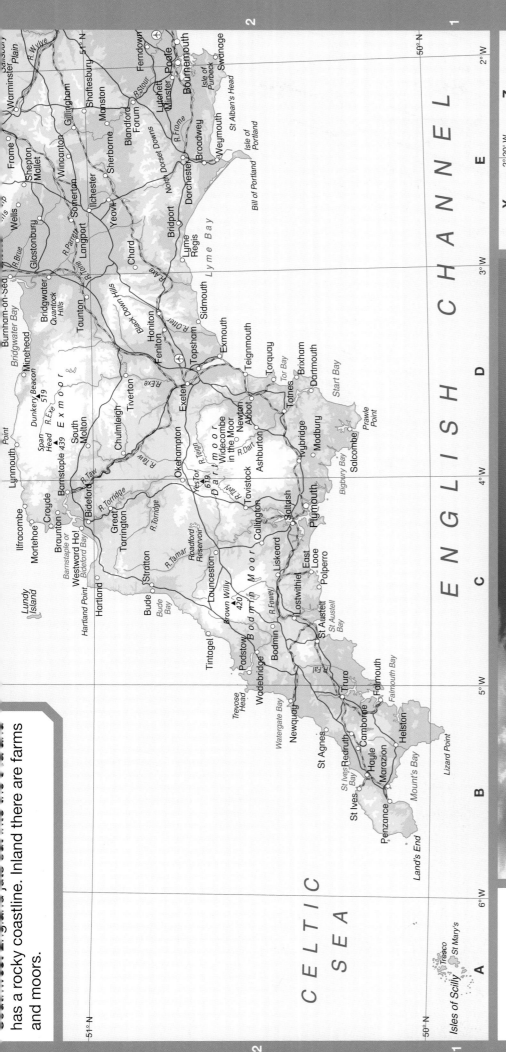

... has a rocky coastline. Inland there are farms and moors.

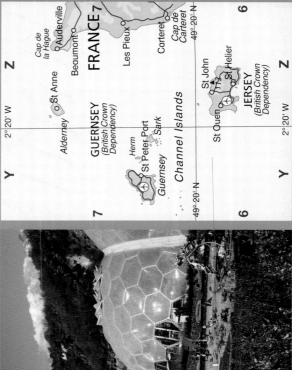

GUERNSEY
(British Crown Dependency)

Alderney
St Anne

Herm
St Peter Port

Guernsey Sark

Channel Islands

49° 20' N

JERSEY
(British Crown Dependency)

St John
St Helier
St Ouen

FRANCE

Cap de la Hague

Auderville
Beaumont

Les Pieux

Carteret
Cap de Carteret

49° 20' N

2° 20' W
2° 20' W

Many tourists visit the Eden Project built in the old clay pits near St Austell. There is a different environment in each of the domes.

Key to symbols

- Country capital
- ○ Main city/town
- ○ Other city/town
- ——— Country boundary
- ——— Road
- ——— Railway
- ✈ Airport
- ◯ Lake
- ◯ River
- ▲ Snowdon Mountain and
  1085 height in metres

Land height above
sea level in metres

over 1500
1000 – 1500
900 – 1000
500 – 900
200 – 500
100 – 200
0 – 100

South and southeast England is the most crowded part of the UK. There are many motorways, railways and airports linking settlements. London dominates the region.

WALES

ENGLAND

Bristol Channel

ENGLISH CHANNEL

Scale : One centimetre on this map is the same as 12.5 kilometres on the ground.

0   25   50   75 km

Grid references: A B C D (top and bottom); 1 2 3 (side)

Selected place names and features:

Penygadair 893, R. Dyfi, Llanfair Caereinion, Shrewsbury, Newport, Wellington, Ashbourne, Belper, Ripley, Eastwood, Ilkeston, Nottingham, Newark-on-Trent, R. Trent, R. Devon, Long Bennington, Sleaford, Holland, R. Witham, Machynlleth, Llanwnog, Welshpool, Telford, Shifnal, Rugeley, Cannock, Uttoxeter, Derby, West Bridgford, Bingham, Grantham, Sutterton, Pinchbeck, Bourne

Cambrian Mts, Newtown, Plynlimon 752, R. Severn, Much Wenlock, Wolverhampton, Codsall, Lichfield, Burton upon Trent, Castle Donnington, Shepshed, Swadlincote, Brownhills, Walsall, Tamworth, Coalville, Kegworth, Loughborough, Mountsorrel, Melton Mowbray, Oakham, Rutland Water, Colsterworth, Market Deeping, Whittles

Rhayader, Great Rhos 660, Llandrindod Wells, Kington, Leominster, Ludlow, Stokesay, Bridgnorth, Brown Clee Hill 540, Kidderminster, Stourbridge, Dudley, West Bromwich, Birmingham, Halesowen, Solihull, Sutton Coldfield, Nuneaton, Hinckley, Coventry, Kenilworth, Rugby, Lutterworth, Market Harborough, Leicester, Oadby, Uppingham, Corby, Oundle, Peterborough, Sawtry, Cho

Claerwen Reservoir, Drygarn Fawr 645, Builth Wells, Hereford, Tenbury Wells, Stourport-on-Severn, R. Teme, Droitwich, Worcester, Bromsgrove, Redditch, Warwick, Royal Leamington Spa, Alcester, Stratford-upon-Avon, Daventry, Wellingborough, Kettering, Burton Latimer, Rounds, Huntingdon, Rushden, Grafham Water, St Neots

Llyn Brianne Reservoir, R. Tywi, Talgarth, Black Mountains 800, Brecon, Great Malvern, Malvern Hills, Evesham, Ledbury, Chipping Campden, Broadway, Banbury, Brackley, Buckingham, Towcester, R. Tove, Northampton, Newport Pagnell, Olney, Bedford, Biggleswade

Glyn-Neath, Hirwaun, Tredegar, Ebbw Vale, Abergavenny, Monmouth, Raglan, Forest of Dean, Newnham, Ross-on-Wye, Dymock, Tewkesbury, Cheltenham, Stow-on-the-Wold, Chipping Norton, Bicester, Milton Keynes, Bletchley, Leighton Buzzard, Woodstock, Aylesbury, Dunstable, Luton, Harpenden, Letchworth, Hitchin, Steve

Neath, Aberdare, Merthyr Tydfil, Blackwood, Newbridge, Pontypool, Cwmbran, Pontypridd, Caerphilly, Newport, Caldicot, Chepstow, Lydney, Berkeley, Stroud, Cirencester, Burford, Witney, Oxford, Kidlington, R. Cherwell, Princes Risborough, Abingdon, Didcot, Chesham, High Wycombe, Hemel Hempstead, St Albans, Hoddesdon, Welwyn Garden City, Watford, Cheshu, Barnet

Port Talbot, Porthcawl, Bridgend, Cowbridge, Penarth, Cardiff, Clevedon, Portishead, Bristol, Mangotsfield, Kingswood, Chipping Sodbury, Malmesbury, Swindon, Stratton St Margaret, Lambourn Downs, Chiltern Hills, Henley-on-Thames, Marlow, Maidenhead, Twyford, Reading, Windsor, Slough, Uxbridge, LONDON, Bro, Croydon, Epsom

Barry, Weston-super-Mare, Chew Valley Lake, Bath, Melksham, Chippenham, Marlborough, R. Kennet, Hungerford, Newbury, Bracknell, Staines-upon-Thames, Wokingham, Camberley, Woking, Gate

Lynmouth, Dunkery Beacon 519, Minehead, Burnham-on-Sea, Bridgwater Bay, Cheddar, Mendip Hills, Wells, Radstock, Frome, Devizes, Trowbridge, Warminster, Upavon, North Tidworth, Salisbury Plain, Andover, Basingstoke, Sandhurst, Fleet, Aldershot, Farnborough, Guildford, Leatherhead, Reigate, Red

R. Exe, Exmoor, Bridgwater, Quantock Hills, Glastonbury, Shepton Mallet, R. Brue, Somerton, Salisbury, Winchester, New Alresford, Alton, Farnham, Godalming, Dorking, Leith Hill 294, Horley

Taunton, Langport, Ilchester, Wincanton, Gillingham, Shaftesbury, Downton, Romsey, Eastleigh, Petersfield, Haslemere, Cranleigh, Billingshurst, Crawley, Grins

Tiverton, Feniton, Honiton, Chard, Yeovil, Sherborne, Manston, Blandford Forum, Ringwood, Lyndhurst, Southampton, Waterlooville, Havant, Chichester, Midhurst, R. Rother, South Downs, Horsham, Haywards Heath, Burgess Hill

Exeter, Topsham, Sidmouth, Black Down Hills, R. Otter, R. Axe, Bridport, Lyme Regis, Dorchester, R. Frome, Lytchett Minster, Poole, Ferndown, Christchurch, Lymington, Brockenhurst, Gosport, Fareham, Portsmouth, Worthing, Hove, Bright, Littlehampton, Bognor Regis

Newton Abbot, Ashburton, Teignmouth, Exmouth, Lyme Bay, Broadwey, Wareham, Bournemouth, Poole Bay, Isle of Purbeck, Yarmouth, Cowes, The Solent, Ryde, Selsey

Torquay, Tor Bay, Weymouth, St Alban's Head, Swanage, The Needles, Newport, Isle of Wight, Shanklin, Foreland

Totnes, Brixham, Dartmouth, Start Bay, Bill of Portland, Isle of Portland, Ventnor, St. Catherine's Point

Prawle Point

E   **F**   **G**   **H**

1° E   2° E   3° E   53° N

Key to symbols

- ■ Capital city
- ● Country capital
- ○ Main city/town
- ∘ Other city/town
- — Country boundary
- — Road
- ╫ Railway
- ✈ Airport
- 〰 Lake
- 〰 River
- ▲ *Leith Hill* Mountain and
- 294 height in metres

Land height above sea level in metres
- over 1500
- 1000 – 1500
- 900 – 1000
- 500 – 900
- 200 – 500
- 100 – 200
- 0 – 100

Land below sea level

NORTH SEA

The Wash

Hunstanton   Wells-next-the-Sea   Cromer
King's Lynn   Fakenham   North Walsham
Narborough   Aylsham
East Dereham   Coltishall
Great R. Ouse   R. Wensum   Hoveton
Downham Market   Swaffham   Norwich   R. Bure
sbech   Wymondham   Norfolk Broads   Great Yarmouth
lington   Southery   Mundford   R. Thet   R. Yare   Corton
Littleport   Loddon   Lowestoft
Ely   Thetford   Long Stratton   Bungay   Kessingland
Soham   Little R. Ouse   Scole   R. Waveney
R. Cam   Stanton   R. Dove   Halesworth
ewmarket   Bury St Edmunds
mbridge   Stowmarket   Saxmundham
N   Haverhill   **D**   Wickham Market   Aldeburgh
Saffron Walden   Sudbury   Claydon   *Orford Ness*
Capel St Mary   Ipswich
Newport   R. Colne   Felixstowe
Braintree   Halstead   R. Stour   Harwich
Bishop's Stortford   Great Dunmow   Coggeshall   Colchester   *The Naze*
arlow   Brightlingsea   Frinton-on-Sea
Chelmsford   Witham   R. Chelmer   Clacton-on-Sea
hipping   Maldon   R. Blackwater
Ongar   Ingatestone   Southminster
Brentwood   R. Crouch   *Foulness Point*
Basildon   Rayleigh
South Ockendon   Southend-on-Sea
River Thames
Tilbury   Grain   Sheerness
Gravesend   Isle of Sheppey
Rochester   Gillingham   Whitstable   Herne Bay   Margate
nley   Chatham   Sittingbourne   *Isle of Thanet*   *North Foreland*
North Downs   Faversham   Broadstairs
Sevenoaks   Maidstone   Chilham   Canterbury   Ramsgate
R. Medway   Gt. R. Stour   Eastry
dge   Royal Tunbridge Wells   Barham   Deal
R. Beult   Ashford   Sellindge   Dover
e   *Weald*   Hamstreet   Folkestone
Crowborough   Hawkhurst   *Romney Marsh*   Hythe
Heathfield   Salehurst   New Romney   *Channel Tunnel*
field   Rye   Lydd   *Dungeness*
Hailsham   *Rye Bay*
olegate   Bexhill   Hastings
aven   Eastbourne
Beachy Head

Strait of Dover

Calais   Gravelines
Coulogne
Guines
FRANCE   St Omer
Wimereux   164 ▲ *Mont des Cats*
Boulogne   Hazebrouck
Desvres   R. Lys

NETHERLANDS
Oosterschelde
Goes
Vlissingen   *Westerschelde*
Westerschelde   Terneuzen
Zeebrugge
Ostend   Bruges
Nieuwpoort
Veurne   **BELGIUM**   Gent
Dunkerque   Diksmuide   Tielt
Yser   IJzer   Roeselare
Ieper   Kortrijk   Oudenaarde
Mouscron   Ronse
Roubaix
Lille   Ath

52° N
51° N

3
2
1

1° E   2° E   3° E

London, one of the world's largest cities, grew up as a port at the lowest crossing on the River Thames.

E   **F**   **G**   **H**

The highest mountains are in the north and west of Great Britain. The south and east are much flatter with low hills. The main rivers such as the Severn, Trent and Thames flow through these areas.

There are mud flats in many river estuaries. These flats are at Applecross in western Scotland.

Key to symbols
- Lake
- River
- ▲ *Ben Nevis* Mountain and 1345 height in metres

Land height above sea level in metres

over 1000	
500 – 1000	
200 – 500	
100 – 200	
0 – 100	

Land below sea level

Total area of the United Kingdom
243 609 sq km

Highest mountain
Ben Nevis 1345 m

ATLANTIC OCEAN

Largest lake
Lough Neagh 396 sq km

Largest island
Great Britain 218 476 sq km

Lowest point
The Fens 4 m below sea level

Longest river (Ireland)
River Shannon 361 km

Longest river (UK)
River Severn 354 km

Hound Tor on Dartmoor is made of old, hard rocks.

Shetland Islands
Mainland
Sumburgh Head

Orkney Islands
Mainland
Hoy
Pentland Firth
Duncansby Head

Cape Wrath

Isle of Lewis

St Kilda

Harris

North Uist

Skye

South Uist

Coll
Tiree

Ben More 966

Mull

Rum

The Minch

Outer Hebrides

Inner Hebrides

North West Highlands

Moray Firth

R. Spey

Loch Ness

Cairngorm Mts

Ben Macdui 1309

R. Dee

Ben Nevis 1345

Grampian Mts

Glen Coe

Loch Tay

R. Tay

Loch Lomond

Ochil Hills

R. Forth

Firth of Forth

North Sea

Jura

Islay

Arran

Firth of Clyde

R. Clyde

Southern Uplands

Merrick 843

R. Tweed

Cheviot Hills

Great

R. Tyne

Great Britain

Malin Head

Donegal Bay

Achill

Lough Mask

Lough Corrib

Galway Bay

R. Foyle

Lower Lough Erne

Antrim Hills

R. Bann

Lough Neagh

Upper Lough Erne

Mourne Mts

Slieve Donard 852

Dundalk Bay

North Channel

Isle of Man

Solway Firth

Scafell Pike 977

Lake District

North York Moors

Flamborough Head

Spurn Head

Ireland

Lough Ree

R. Shannon

R. Boyne

Lough Derg

Lugnaquilla Mtn 926

R. Barrow

Wicklow Mts

R. Suir

Carrauntoohil 1041

R. Blackwater

Cape Clear

Irish Sea

Anglesey

Snowdon 1085

R. Dee

R. Mersey

High Peak
Kinder Scout 636

Pennines

R. Tees

R. Ouse

The Wash

Norfolk Broads

Cardigan Bay

St George's Channel

St David's Head

Cambrian Mountains

R. Trent

R. Severn

R. Great Ouse

The Fens

R. Wye

Black Mountains 886

Brecon Beacons

R. Avon

R. Severn

Cotswold Hills

R. Thames

Chiltern Hills

R. Thames

Celtic Sea

Bristol Channel

Mendip Hills

Exmoor

North Downs

South Downs

Beachy Head

Bodmin Moor

Dartmoor
Yes Tor 619

R. Tamar

Lyme Bay

Isle of Wight

Land's End

Start Point

English Channel

Channel Islands

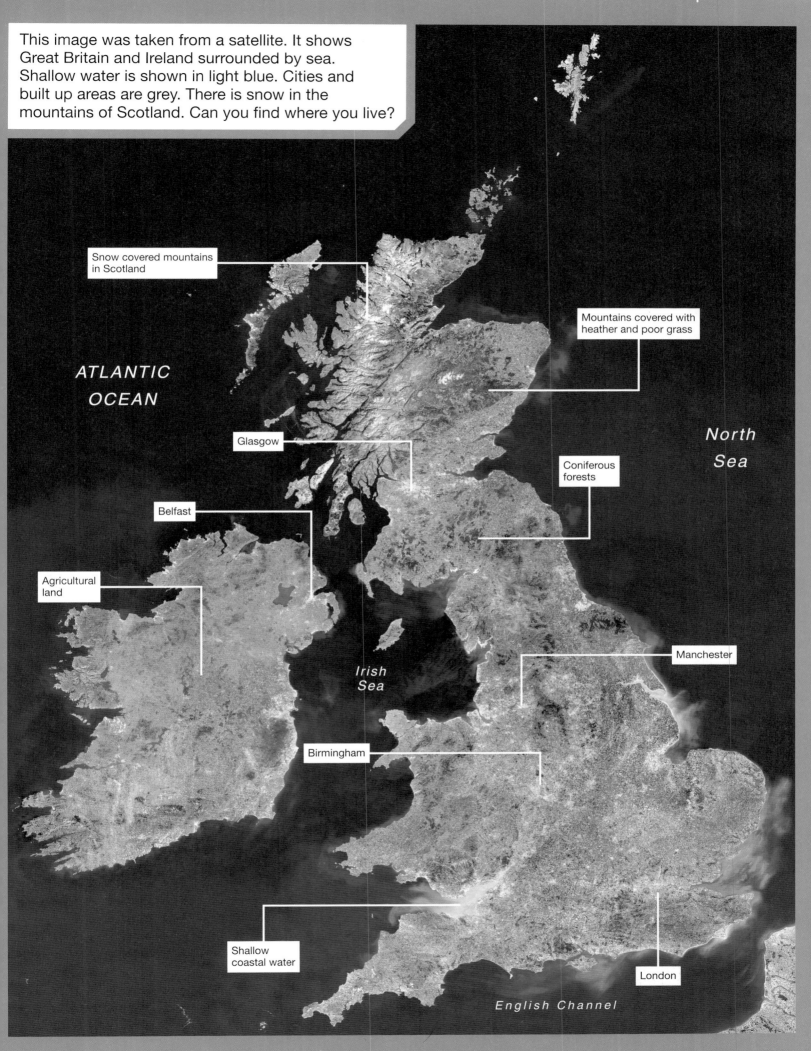

This image was taken from a satellite. It shows Great Britain and Ireland surrounded by sea. Shallow water is shown in light blue. Cities and built up areas are grey. There is snow in the mountains of Scotland. Can you find where you live?

Snow covered mountains in Scotland

Mountains covered with heather and poor grass

ATLANTIC OCEAN

North Sea

Glasgow

Coniferous forests

Belfast

Agricultural land

Manchester

Irish Sea

Birmingham

Shallow coastal water

London

English Channel

The mixture of sun, rain and wind make the weather.

Extreme weather causes problems. In December 2015 torrential rain flooded York and other parts of England.

Annual rainfall

All parts of the UK have rain throughout the year. Western areas are the wettest. Here winds from the sea shed water as they rise over the mountains.

Average annual rainfall
- more than 2000 mm
- 1500 – 2000 mm
- 1000 – 1500 mm
- 750 – 1000 mm
- 625 – 750 mm
- less than 625 mm
- Location of places on climate graphs

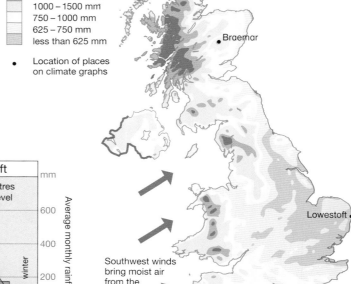

Southwest winds bring moist air from the Atlantic Ocean

Seasonal climate graphs

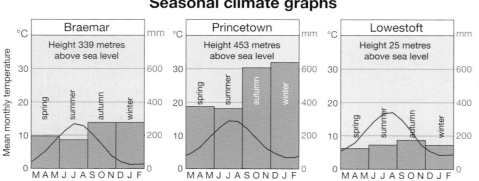

Braemar — Height 339 metres above sea level
Princetown — Height 453 metres above sea level
Lowestoft — Height 25 metres above sea level

Winter temperatures

In January, warm ocean currents bring milder conditions to the southwest of the UK. The coldest areas are the mountains in the north.

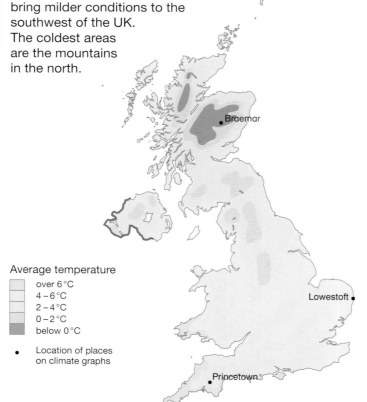

Average temperature
- over 6 °C
- 4 – 6 °C
- 2 – 4 °C
- 0 – 2 °C
- below 0 °C
- Location of places on climate graphs

Summer temperatures

In July, the warmest parts of the UK are in the south, especially along the coasts. Mountain areas are the coolest.

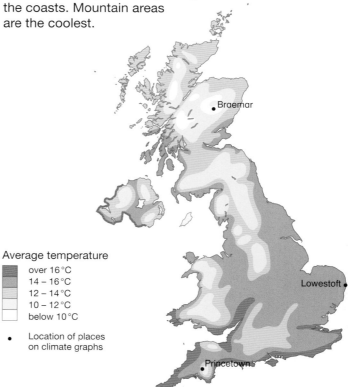

Average temperature
- over 16 °C
- 14 – 16 °C
- 12 – 14 °C
- 10 – 12 °C
- below 10 °C
- Location of places on climate graphs

Some parts of the UK are much more crowded than others. London and big cities such as Birmingham, Leeds and Glasgow are the most crowded areas. Hill and mountain areas are the emptiest.

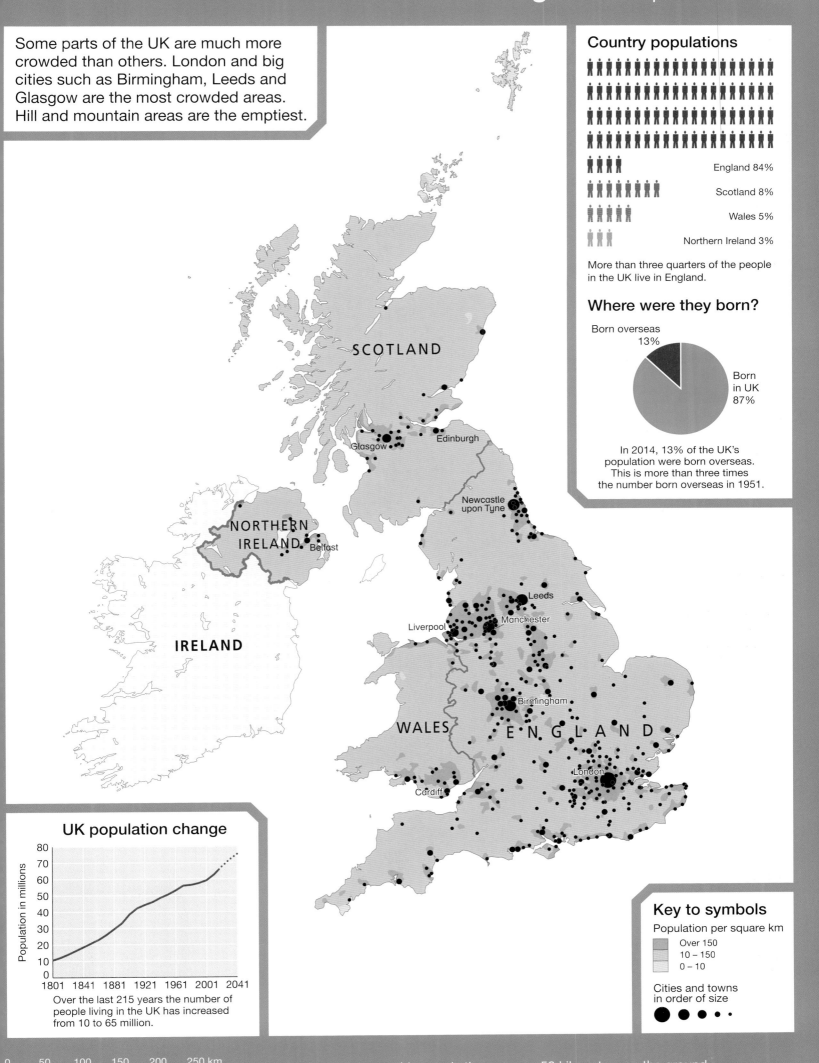

Country populations

England 84%

Scotland 8%

Wales 5%

Northern Ireland 3%

More than three quarters of the people in the UK live in England.

Where were they born?

Born overseas 13%

Born in UK 87%

In 2014, 13% of the UK's population were born overseas. This is more than three times the number born overseas in 1951.

SCOTLAND

Glasgow   Edinburgh

NORTHERN IRELAND   Belfast

Newcastle upon Tyne

IRELAND

Leeds

Liverpool   Manchester

Birmingham

WALES   E N G L A N D

Cardiff   London

UK population change

Population in millions

80
70
60
50
40
30
20
10
0

1801 1841 1881 1921 1961 2001 2041

Over the last 215 years the number of people living in the UK has increased from 10 to 65 million.

Key to symbols

Population per square km

Over 150

10 – 150

0 – 10

Cities and towns in order of size

0   50   100   150   200   250 km

Scale : One centimetre on this map is the same as 50 kilometres on the ground.

The landscape and climate have a big influence on UK farming. In the mountains of Scotland and Wales many farmers keep sheep. The flatter, drier lands in the south and east of England tend to be planted with growing crops or are used for grazing cows.

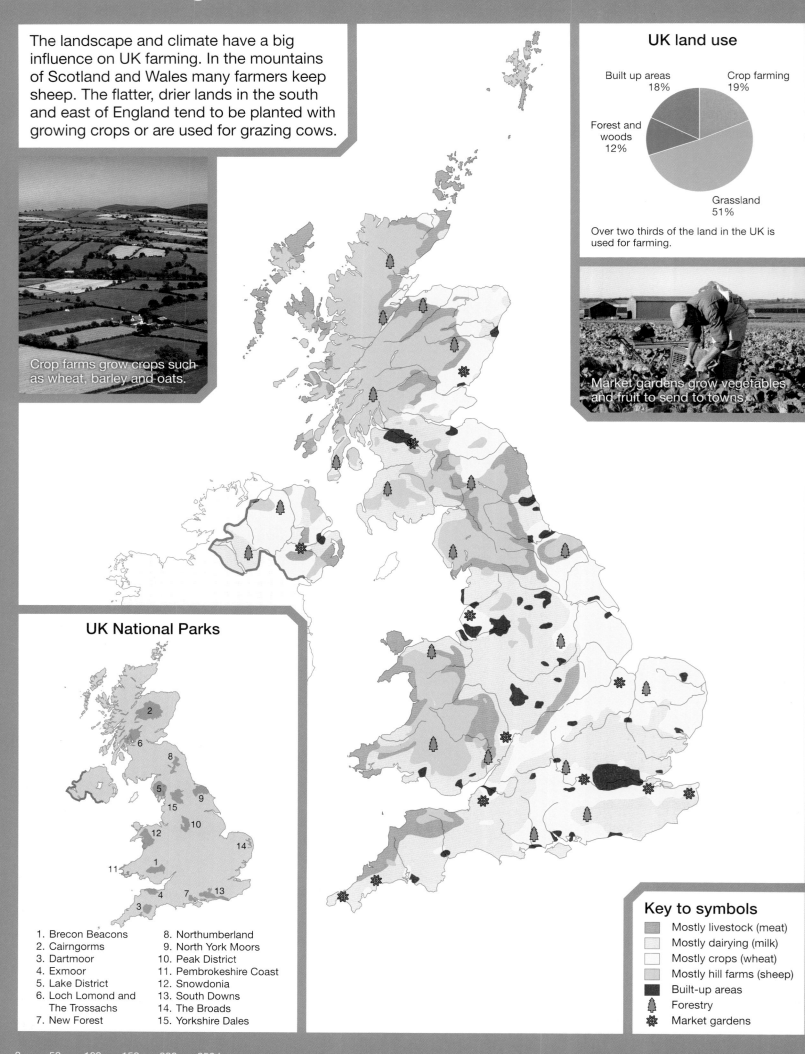

Crop farms grow crops such as wheat, barley and oats.

UK land use

Built up areas 18%
Crop farming 19%
Forest and woods 12%
Grassland 51%

Over two thirds of the land in the UK is used for farming.

Market gardens grow vegetables and fruit to send to towns.

UK National Parks

1. Brecon Beacons
2. Cairngorms
3. Dartmoor
4. Exmoor
5. Lake District
6. Loch Lomond and The Trossachs
7. New Forest
8. Northumberland
9. North York Moors
10. Peak District
11. Pembrokeshire Coast
12. Snowdonia
13. South Downs
14. The Broads
15. Yorkshire Dales

Key to symbols

Mostly livestock (meat)
Mostly dairying (milk)
Mostly crops (wheat)
Mostly hill farms (sheep)
Built-up areas
Forestry
Market gardens

0   50   100   150   200   250 km

Scale : One centimetre on this map is the same as 50 kilometres on the ground.

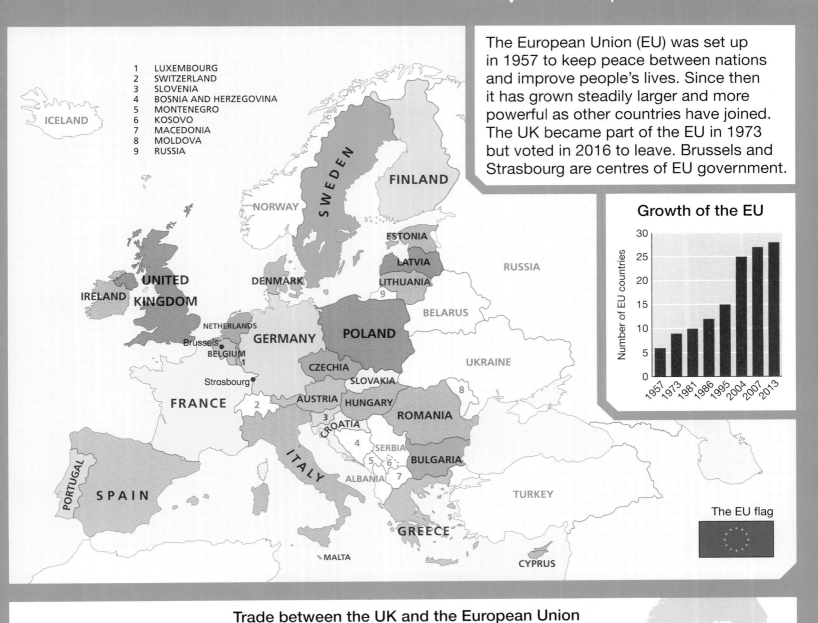

1 LUXEMBOURG
2 SWITZERLAND
3 SLOVENIA
4 BOSNIA AND HERZEGOVINA
5 MONTENEGRO
6 KOSOVO
7 MACEDONIA
8 MOLDOVA
9 RUSSIA

The European Union (EU) was set up in 1957 to keep peace between nations and improve people's lives. Since then it has grown steadily larger and more powerful as other countries have joined. The UK became part of the EU in 1973 but voted in 2016 to leave. Brussels and Strasbourg are centres of EU government.

Growth of the EU

The EU flag

Trade between the UK and the European Union

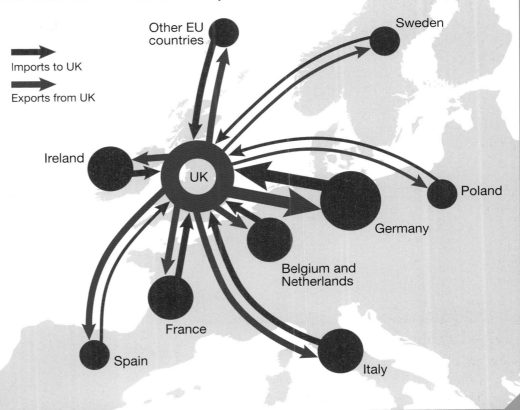

Over half the UK's trade is with European Union (EU) countries. The map shows imports and exports between the UK and the EU. Germany is the UK's biggest trading partner. The UK also has worldwide trade links with the USA, China and countries in other continents.

Imports to UK

Exports from UK

Most manufactured goods are shipped in containers.

A B C D E F G H I J K L

There are around 50 countries in Europe. Ukraine and France are the largest. Malta and Andorra are two of the smallest. Both Turkey and Russia are split between Europe and Asia.

Total population of Europe
(excluding Russia)
595 million

Russia
Area 17 million sq km
Population 143 million

ARCTIC OCEAN

Jan Mayen (Norway)

Novaya Zemlya

Arctic Circle

70° N

Arctic Circle

ICELAND
■ Reykjavik

ATLANTIC

Country with most people
(excluding Russia)
Germany 81 million

OCEAN

60° N

Faroe Islands (Denmark)

NORWAY

SWEDEN

FINLAND

White Sea

RUSSIA

Helsinki ○ St Petersburg

Oslo ■

Stockholm ■

Tallinn
ESTONIA

■ Moscow

North Sea

Edinburgh ○

Belfast ○

UNITED

Dublin ●
IRELAND

KINGDOM

LATVIA
Riga ■

Baltic Sea

LITHUANIA
Vilnius ■

RUSSIA

Minsk ■

BELARUS

Largest country
(excluding Russia)
Ukraine 603 700 sq km

50° N

London ■

English Channel

1
DENMARK
Copenhagen ■

Berlin ■

Warsaw ■

GERMANY

POLAND

Prague ■

Kiev ■

UKRAINE

Volgograd ○

2

3

CZECHIA

Largest city
(Western Europe)
Paris 11 million

■ Paris

Munich ○

Vienna ■

SLOVAKIA
Bratislava ■

MOLDOVA

Chișinău ■

Caspian Sea

FRANCE

4 5

AUSTRIA

Budapest ■

HUNGARY

ROMANIA

Odesa ○

Bay of Biscay

Lyon ○

Milan ○

6

Zagreb ■

Belgrade ■

Bucharest ■

Black Sea

SAN MARINO

CROATIA

7

SERBIA

PORTUGAL

ANDORRA

MONACO

Corsica

ITALY

Adriatic Sea

8 9

BULGARIA
Sofia ■

40° N

Lisbon ■

Madrid ■

Barcelona ○

Rome ■

Skopje ●

Istanbul ○

Largest city
Istanbul 12 million

SPAIN

Balearic Islands

Palma de Mallorca ○

Sardinia

Tirana ●
ALBANIA

10

TURKEY

Gibraltar (UK)

Strait of Gibraltar

Sicily

GREECE

Aegean Sea

30° N

Crete

Rhodes

ASIA

Mediterranean Sea

Athens ■

AFRICA

MALTA

N
W E
S

The Kremlin and other ancient buildings around Red Square, Moscow, are the heart of Russia.

Key to symbols

◢ Countries
■ Capital city
○ Important city/town

0 250 500 750 1000 1250 1500 km

Scale : One centimetre on this map is the same as 250 kilometres on the ground.

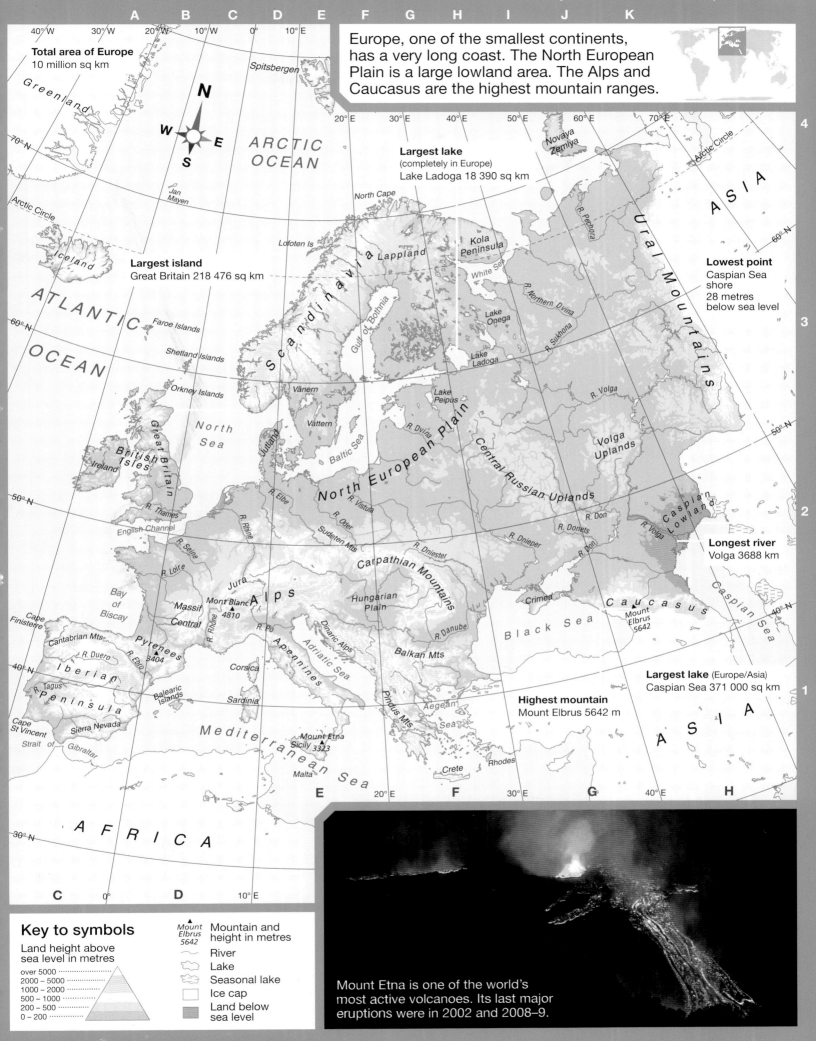

Europe, one of the smallest continents, has a very long coast. The North European Plain is a large lowland area. The Alps and Caucasus are the highest mountain ranges.

Total area of Europe
10 million sq km

ARCTIC OCEAN

Largest lake
(completely in Europe)
Lake Ladoga 18 390 sq km

Largest island
Great Britain 218 476 sq km

ATLANTIC OCEAN

Lowest point
Caspian Sea shore
28 metres below sea level

Longest river
Volga 3688 km

Largest lake (Europe/Asia)
Caspian Sea 371 000 sq km

Highest mountain
Mount Elbrus 5642 m

ASIA

Greenland

Spitsbergen

Jan Mayen

Iceland

Arctic Circle

Faroe Islands

Shetland Islands

Orkney Islands

North Sea

Great Britain

British Isles

Ireland

R. Thames

English Channel

Bay of Biscay

Cape Finisterre

Cantabrian Mts

R. Duero

Iberian Peninsula

R. Tagus

Cape St Vincent

Sierra Nevada

Strait of Gibraltar

AFRICA

Massif Central

R. Seine

R. Loire

Jura

Mont Blanc 4810

Alps

Pyrenees 3404

R. Ebro

R. Rhône

R. Rhine

R. Elbe

R. Oder

Corsica

Balearic Islands

Sardinia

Apennines

Dinaric Alps

Adriatic Sea

Mount Etna Sicily 3323

Malta

Mediterranean Sea

North Cape

Lofoten Is

Scandinavia

Lappland

Gulf of Bothnia

Vänern

Vättern

Jutland

Baltic Sea

R. Vistula

Sudeten Mts

Carpathian Mountains

Hungarian Plain

R. Po

R. Danube

Balkan Mts

Pindus Mts

Aegean Sea

Crete

Rhodes

Novaya Zemlya

Kola Peninsula

White Sea

Lake Onega

Lake Ladoga

Lake Peipus

R. Dvina

R. Northern Dvina

R. Pechora

R. Sukhona

North European Plain

Central Russian Uplands

R. Dniester

R. Dnieper

R. Donets

R. Don

R. Don

Crimea

Black Sea

R. Volga

Volga Uplands

R. Volga

Caspian Lowland

Caspian Sea

Ural Mountains

Caucasus

Mount Elbrus 5642

ASIA

Key to symbols

Land height above sea level in metres

over 5000	
2000 – 5000	
1000 – 2000	
500 – 1000	
200 – 500	
0 – 200	

Mount Elbrus 5642 ▲ Mountain and height in metres

∿ River

Lake

Seasonal lake

Ice cap

Land below sea level

Mount Etna is one of the world's most active volcanoes. Its last major eruptions were in 2002 and 2008–9.

0   250   500   750   1000   1250   1500 km

Scale : One centimetre on this map is the same as 250 kilometres on the ground.

A   B   C   D   E   F   G   H   I   J

Three Scandinavian countries – Norway, Sweden and Denmark – lie at the heart of Northern Europe. The people who live in these countries have similar traditions and beliefs which date back to Viking times. There are also links between their languages.

10°E   15°E   20°E

65°N   Arctic Circle   20°W   15°W   10°W   5°W   0°   5°E

N
W   E
S

Tromsø

ICELAND
Akureyri
Reykjavik   Vatnajökull
Seyðisfjörður

Lofoten Islands

Narvik

Bodø

60°N

Norwegian
Sea

Trondheim

Umeå

Faroe
Islands
(Denmark)

Ålesund

Östersund

Sundsvall

Galdhøpiggen
2470
Lillehammer

Shetland
Islands

Bergen

Gulf of Bothnia

Uppsala

4

Orkney
Islands

Drammen   Oslo
Stavanger   Karlstad   Örebro   Västerås   Stockholm

ATLANTIC

Outer Hebrides

Inverness

North
Sea

Kristiansand

Norrköping

OCEAN

Ben
Nevis
1345   Grampian Mountains   Aberdeen

Vänern   Jönköping   Gotland

55°N

Glasgow   Dundee

Skagerrak   Gothenburg   Vättern

Edinburgh

Aalborg   Kattegat   Halmstad   Öland

Londonderry
(Derry)   Belfast   Carlisle   Newcastle upon Tyne

DENMARK

Karlskrona

UNITED

Aarhus

3

Galway   IRELAND   KINGDOM
Limerick   Irish Sea   Blackpool   Leeds
Dublin   Liverpool
Manchester
Cork   Wexford   Sheffield
Birmingham   Nottingham

Esbjerg   Odense   Copenhagen   Malmö

Bornholm

Baltic

Gdańsk

Koszalin

Kiel

Swansea   Norwich
Cardiff   Oxford   R. Thames
Bristol   London

NETHERLANDS
Amsterdam
The Hague   IJsselmeer
Rotterdam

Rostock

Szczecin

Hamburg

Bydgoszcz

Groningen

Bremen

R. Elbe

Hannover   Magdeburg   Berlin

POLA

Poznań

50°N

Plymouth   Southampton
Dover
Strait of Dover   Bruges
Calais

Bielefeld

R. Oder

Zielona
Góra   Wrocław

Channel
Islands   Le Havre   Amiens
Rouen

Eindhoven   Duisburg
Dortmund
Antwerp   Essen   Düsseldorf
BELGIUM   Brussels   Cologne
Lille   Liège   Bonn

GERMANY

Leipzig   Dresden

Sudeten Mts   Katow

2

Brest   Caen

LUXEMBOURG
Luxembourg

Erfurt

Prague

Ostrava

English Channel

Rennes   Le Mans   Reims
Paris

Frankfurt
Mainz

Nuremberg

CZECHIA
(CZECH REPUBLIC)   Plzeň

Brno

SLO

Nancy   R. Rhine   Karlsruhe
Orléans   Strasbourg   Stuttgart

Vienna

Bratislav

45°N   5°W

Nantes   R. Loire
Tours
FRANCE
La Rochelle   Poitiers

R. Loire
R. Seine   Dijon   Basel   R. Danube   Linz
Zürich   Munich   R. Inn

Salzburg

AUSTRIA

Budapest

5°E   10°E   15°E

E   F   G   H   I   J

0   100   200   300   400   500   600 km

Scale : One centimetre on this map is the same as 100 kilometres on the ground.

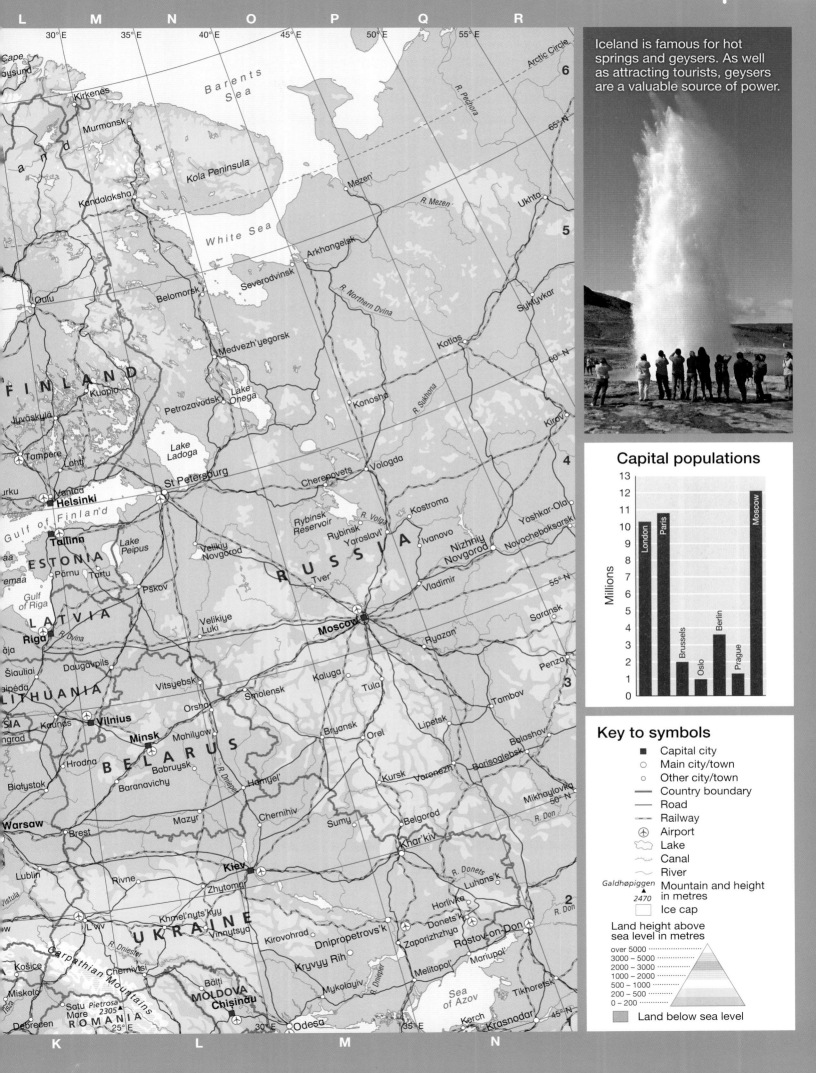

The Mediterranean Sea links many of the countries of southern Europe. In the past, the Romans and Ancient Greeks both had empires here. Today, good summer weather makes the Mediterranean popular for holidays.

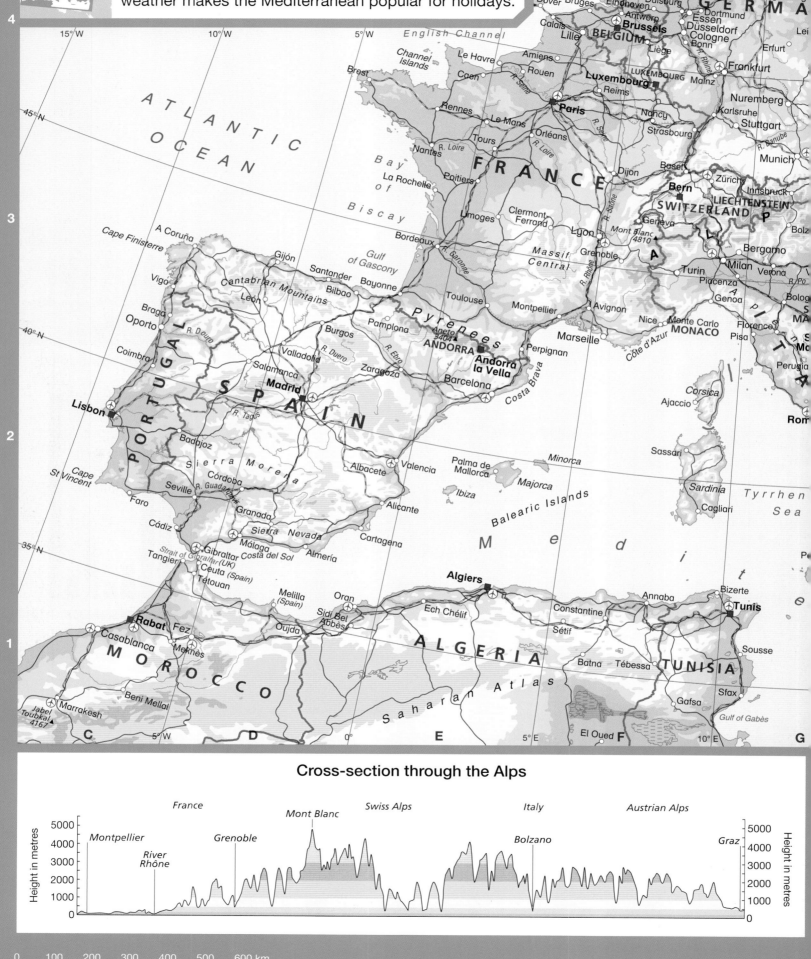

Cross-section through the Alps

Scale : One centimetre on this map is the same as 100 kilometres on the ground.

0 100 200 300 400 500 600 km

Key to symbols

- ■ Capital city
- ○ Main city/town
- ○ Other city/town
- —— Country boundary
- —— Road
- —·— Railway
- ✈ Airport
- Lake
- Seasonal lake
- River
- *Mont Blanc* 4810 ▲ Mountain and height in metres

Land height above sea level in metres

- over 5000
- 3000 – 5000
- 2000 – 3000
- 1000 – 2000
- 500 – 1000
- 200 – 500
- 0 – 200

Land below sea level

The Alps divide Europe with a wall of rock and ice 1000 km long.

Capital populations

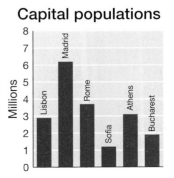

Capital populations bar chart showing Millions (0–8) for: Lisbon, Madrid, Rome, Sofia, Athens, Bucharest.

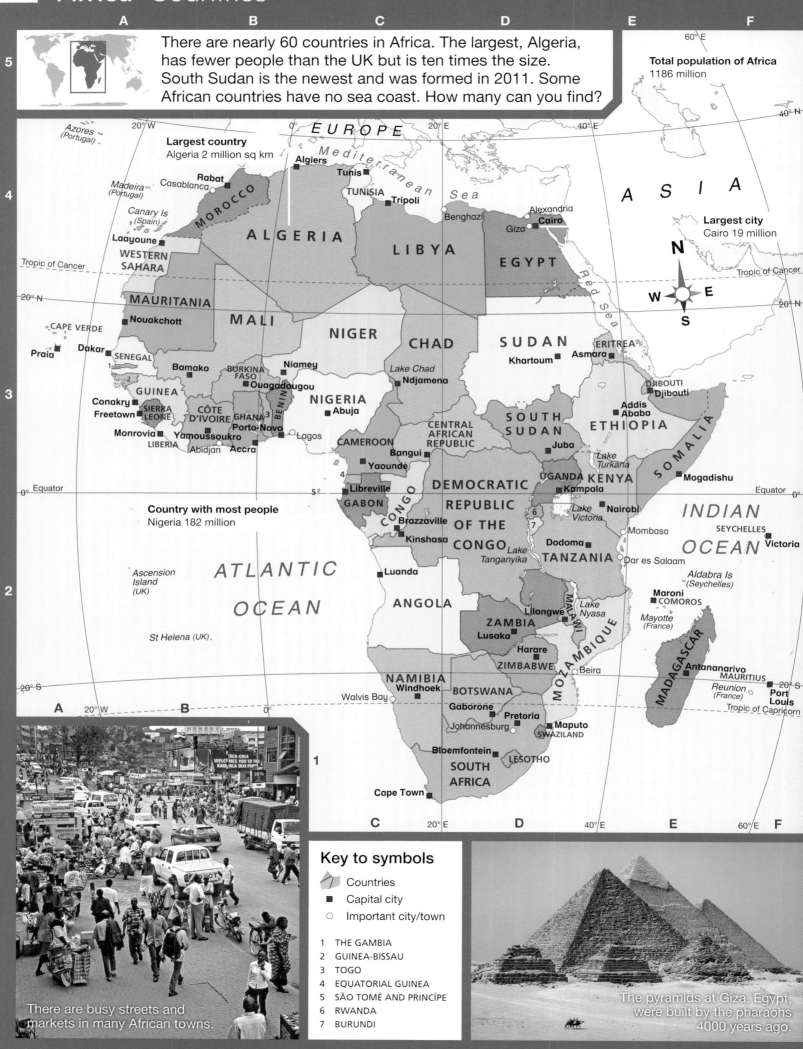

There are nearly 60 countries in Africa. The largest, Algeria, has fewer people than the UK but is ten times the size. South Sudan is the newest and was formed in 2011. Some African countries have no sea coast. How many can you find?

Total population of Africa
1186 million

Largest country
Algeria 2 million sq km

Largest city
Cairo 19 million

Country with most people
Nigeria 182 million

EUROPE

ASIA

Mediterranean Sea

Red Sea

ATLANTIC OCEAN

INDIAN OCEAN

Azores (Portugal)
Madeira (Portugal)
Canary Is (Spain)
Tropic of Cancer
CAPE VERDE
Praia
Ascension Island (UK)
St Helena (UK)

MOROCCO
Algiers
Tunis
Tripoli
TUNISIA
Rabat
Casablanca
Laayoune
WESTERN SAHARA
ALGERIA
LIBYA
EGYPT
Benghazi
Alexandria
Giza
Cairo

MAURITANIA
Nouakchott
MALI
NIGER
CHAD
SUDAN
Khartoum
Asmara
ERITREA
DJIBOUTI
Djibouti

Dakar
SENEGAL
Bamako
BURKINA FASO
Niamey
Ouagadougou
Lake Chad
Ndjamena
NIGERIA
Abuja
CENTRAL AFRICAN REPUBLIC
SOUTH SUDAN
Juba
Addis Ababa
ETHIOPIA
SOMALIA

GUINEA
Conakry
Freetown
SIERRA LEONE
CÔTE D'IVOIRE
GHANA
Porto-Novo
Lagos
Monrovia
Yamoussoukro
Abidjan
Accra
LIBERIA
BENIN
CAMEROON
Bangui
Yaoundé

Libreville
GABON
CONGO
Brazzaville
Kinshasa
DEMOCRATIC REPUBLIC OF THE CONGO
UGANDA
Kampala
KENYA
Nairobi
Lake Victoria
Lake Turkana
Mogadishu

Luanda
ANGOLA
Lake Tanganyika
Dodoma
TANZANIA
Dar es Salaam
Mombasa
SEYCHELLES
Victoria
Aldabra Is (Seychelles)

ZAMBIA
Lusaka
Lilongwe
MALAWI
Lake Nyasa
COMOROS
Maroni
Mayotte (France)

Harare
ZIMBABWE
MOZAMBIQUE
Beira
MADAGASCAR
Antananarivo
MAURITIUS
Port Louis
Reunion (France)

NAMIBIA
Windhoek
Walvis Bay
BOTSWANA
Gaborone
Pretoria
Johannesburg
Maputo
SWAZILAND
Bloemfontein
LESOTHO
SOUTH AFRICA
Cape Town

Equator
Tropic of Capricorn

Key to symbols

◩ Countries
■ Capital city
○ Important city/town

1 THE GAMBIA
2 GUINEA-BISSAU
3 TOGO
4 EQUATORIAL GUINEA
5 SÃO TOMÉ AND PRINCÍPE
6 RWANDA
7 BURUNDI

There are busy streets and markets in many African towns.

The pyramids at Giza, Egypt, were built by the pharaohs 4000 years ago.

0   450   900   1350   1800   2250   2700 km

Scale : One centimetre on this map is the same as 450 kilometres on the ground.

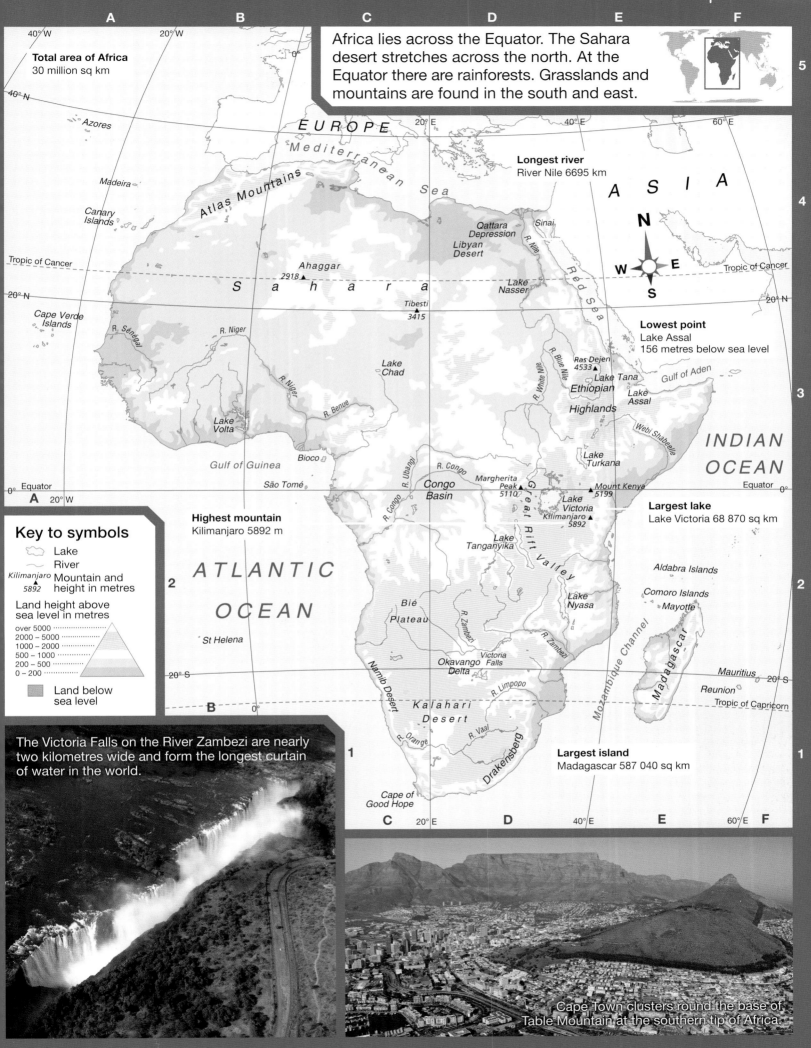

A B C D E F

40° W 20° W 20° E 40° E 60° E

Total area of Africa
30 million sq km

Africa lies across the Equator. The Sahara desert stretches across the north. At the Equator there are rainforests. Grasslands and mountains are found in the south and east.

40° N

Azores

Madeira

Canary Islands

EUROPE

Mediterranean Sea

Atlas Mountains

Tropic of Cancer

20° N

Cape Verde Islands

R. Sénégal

S a h a r a

Ahaggar
2918 ▲

Tibesti
3415

ASIA

N
W · E
S

Longest river
River Nile 6695 km

Qattara
Depression
Libyan
Desert

Sinai

R. Nile

Lake
Nasser

Red Sea

Tropic of Cancer

20° N

R. Niger

R. Niger

R. Benue

Lake
Chad

Lake
Volta

Gulf of Guinea

Bioco

São Tomé

Equator
0°
A
20° W

Highest mountain
Kilimanjaro 5892 m

ATLANTIC

OCEAN

St Helena

Key to symbols

⌇ Lake
〜 River
Kilimanjaro ▲ Mountain and
5892 height in metres

Land height above
sea level in metres
over 5000
2000 – 5000
1000 – 2000
500 – 1000
200 – 500
0 – 200

Land below
sea level

R. Congo

R. Ubangi

R. Congo

Congo
Basin

Margherita
Peak
5110 ▲

Great Rift Valley

Lake
Tanganyika

Bié
Plateau

R. Zambezi

Lake
Victoria

Kilimanjaro
5892 ▲

Lake
Nyasa

R. Zambezi

Victoria Falls

Okavango
Delta

Namib Desert

R. Orange

R. Vaal

K a l a h a r i
D e s e r t

R. Limpopo

Drakensberg

Cape of
Good Hope

C
20° E

D
40° E

Ras Dejen
4533 ▲
Lake Tana

Ethiopian

Highlands

Gulf of Aden

Lake
Assal

Webi Shabeelle

Lake
Turkana

Mount Kenya
▲ 5199

INDIAN

OCEAN

Lowest point
Lake Assal
156 metres below sea level

Largest lake
Lake Victoria 68 870 sq km

Aldabra Islands

Comoro Islands
Mayotte

Madagascar

Mozambique Channel

Mauritius

Reunion

Tropic of Capricorn

Largest island
Madagascar 587 040 sq km

E
40° E

F
60° E

20° S

0°

5

4

3

2

1

The Victoria Falls on the River Zambezi are nearly two kilometres wide and form the longest curtain of water in the world.

Cape Town clusters round the base of Table Mountain at the southern tip of Africa.

0 450 900 1350 1800 2250 2700 km

Scale : One centimetre on this map is the same as 450 kilometres on the ground.

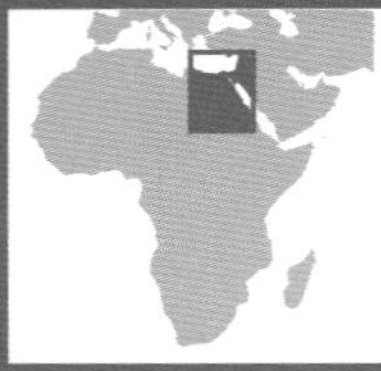

Egypt is one of the oldest countries in the world. Today it has a population of 92 million. Most people live in the valley of the River Nile. The capital, Cairo, is larger than London.

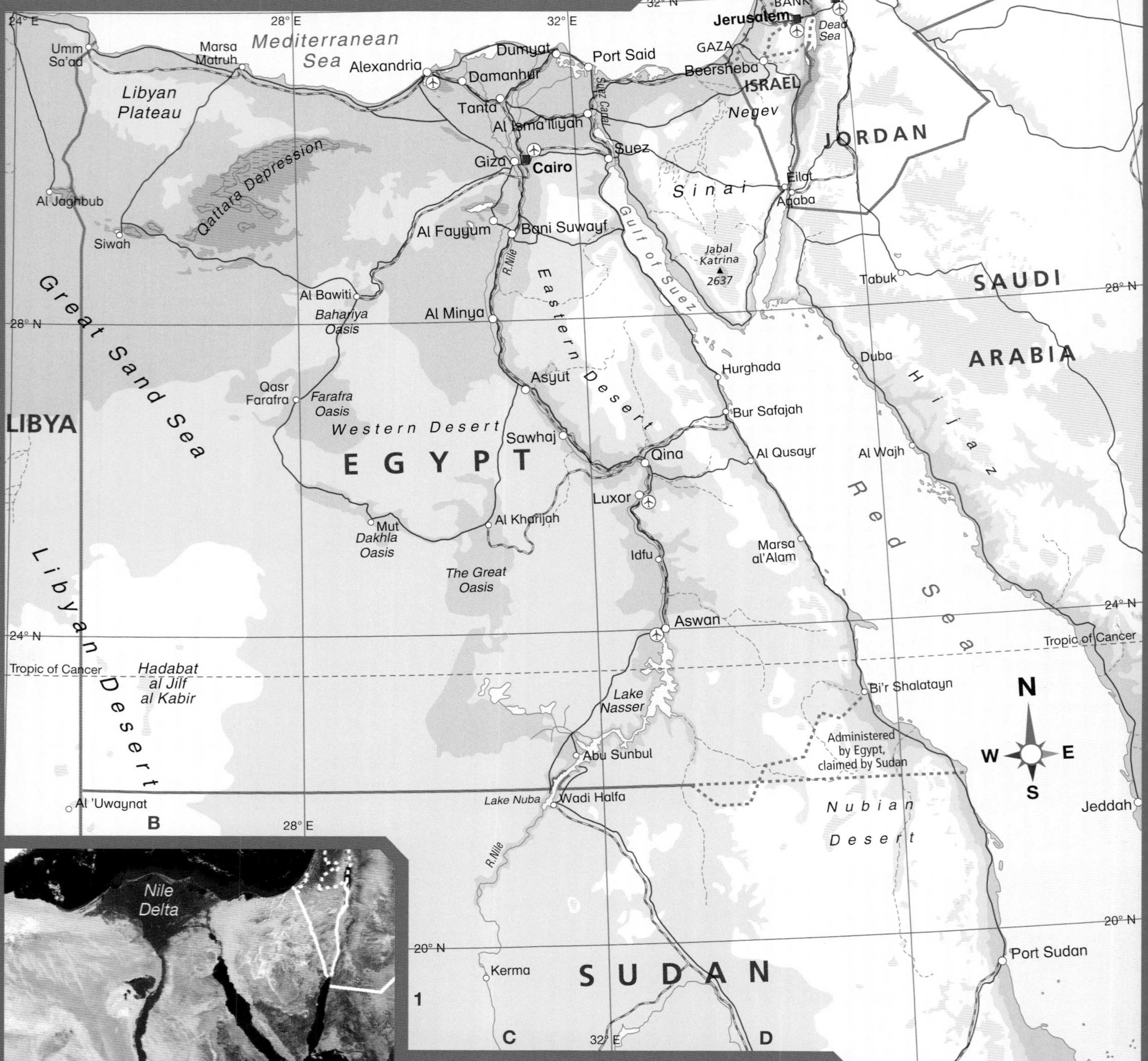

Grid references: A B C D E (columns) / 1 2 3 4 5 (rows)

Coordinates: 24° E, 28° E, 32° E, 36° E, 40° E / 32° N, 28° N, 24° N, 20° N

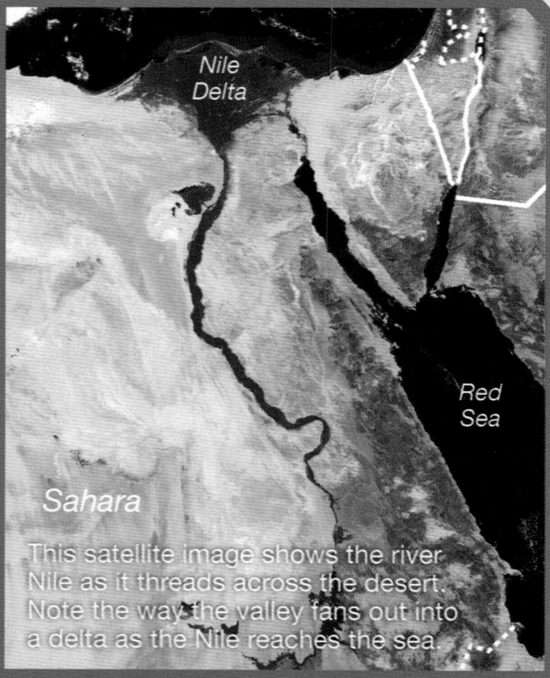

SYRIA
Damascus
Haifa
Sea of Galilee
Tel Aviv-Yafo
WEST BANK
Amman
Irbid
Jerusalem
GAZA
Beersheba
ISRAEL
Negev
Dead Sea
JORDAN
Sinai
Eilat
Aqaba
Tabuk
SAUDI ARABIA
Jabal Katrina 2637
Duba
Hijaz
Al Wajh
Red Sea
Jeddah
Port Sudan

Mediterranean Sea
Umm Sa'ad
Marsa Matruh
Alexandria
Dumyat
Damanhur
Port Said
Libyan Plateau
Tanta
Al Isma'iliyah
Suez Canal
Qattara Depression
Giza
Cairo
Suez
Gulf of Suez
Al Jaghbub
Al Fayyum
Bani Suwayf
Hurghada
Siwah
R. Nile
Eastern Desert
Bur Safajah
Great Sand Sea
Al Bawiti
Bahariya Oasis
Al Minya
LIBYA
Qasr Farafra
Farafra Oasis
Asyut
Western Desert
EGYPT
Sawhaj
Qina
Al Qusayr
Luxor
Marsa al'Alam
Mut Dakhla Oasis
Al Kharijah
Idfu
The Great Oasis
Libyan Desert
Aswan
Tropic of Cancer
Hadabat al Jilf al Kabir
Lake Nasser
Bi'r Shalatayn
Administered by Egypt, claimed by Sudan
Abu Sunbul
Nubian Desert
Al 'Uwaynat
Lake Nuba
Wadi Halfa
R. Nile
Kerma
SUDAN

Compass: N, W, E, S

Satellite image caption:
Nile Delta
Red Sea
Sahara
This satellite image shows the river Nile as it threads across the desert. Note the way the valley fans out into a delta as the Nile reaches the sea.

Key to symbols

■	Capital city
○	Main city/town
○	Other city/town
—	Country boundary
—	Road
Railway	Railway
✈	Airport
Lake	Lake
Seasonal lake	Seasonal lake
Canal	Canal
River	River
Jabal Katrina ▲ 2637	Mountain and height in metres

Land height above sea level in metres
over 5000
3000 – 5000
2000 – 3000
1000 – 2000
500 – 1000
200 – 500
0 – 200
Land below sea level

Facts about Egypt

Area	1 million sq km
Highest peak	Jabal Katrina 2637 m
Longest river	Nile 6695 km
Largest lake	L. Nasser 5248 sq km
Population	92 million
Largest city	Cairo 19 million

0 100 200 300 400 500 km

Scale : One centimetre on this map is the same as 75 kilometres on the ground.

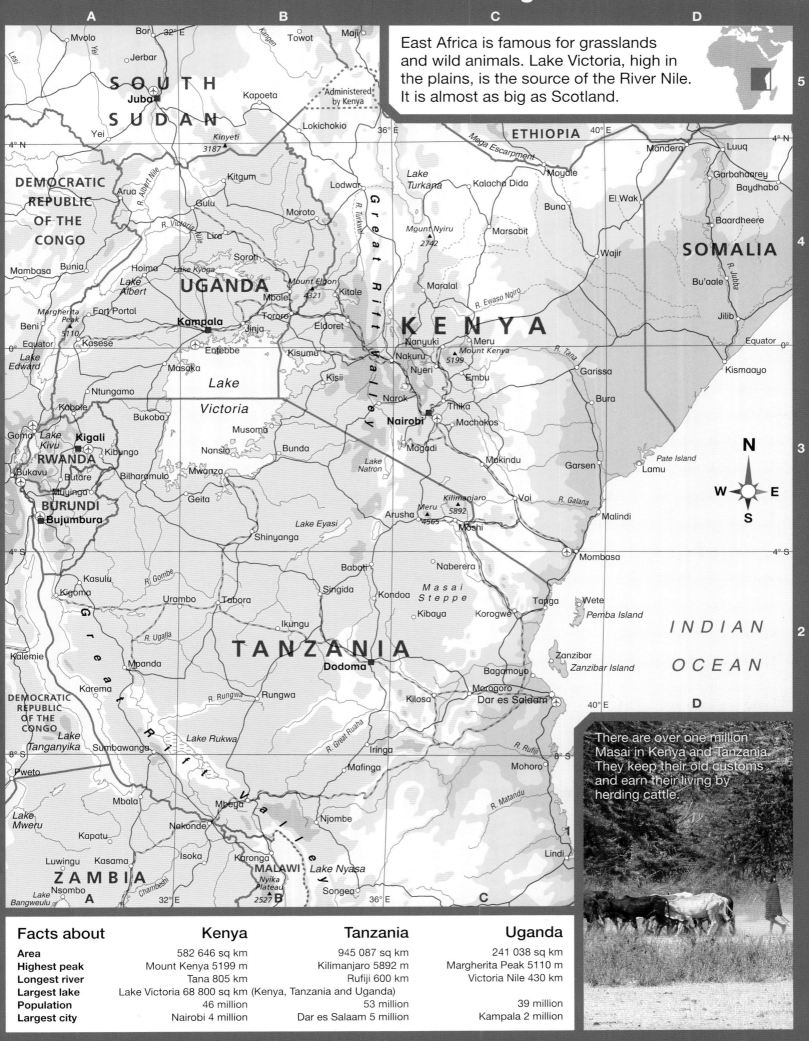

East Africa is famous for grasslands and wild animals. Lake Victoria, high in the plains, is the source of the River Nile. It is almost as big as Scotland.

There are over one million Masai in Kenya and Tanzania. They keep their old customs and earn their living by herding cattle.

Facts about	Kenya	Tanzania	Uganda
Area	582 646 sq km	945 087 sq km	241 038 sq km
Highest peak	Mount Kenya 5199 m	Kilimanjaro 5892 m	Margherita Peak 5110 m
Longest river	Tana 805 km	Rufiji 600 km	Victoria Nile 430 km
Largest lake	Lake Victoria 68 800 sq km (Kenya, Tanzania and Uganda)		
Population	46 million	53 million	39 million
Largest city	Nairobi 4 million	Dar es Salaam 5 million	Kampala 2 million

0   100   200   300   400   500 km

Scale : One centimetre on this map is the same as 80 kilometres on the ground.

There are 49 countries in Asia. India, China and Russia are the largest. Singapore is the smallest. Some are islands. See how many you can find on the map.

Total population of Asia
(including Russia)
4538 million

Russia
Area 17 million sq km
Population 143 million

Country with most people
China 1384 million

Largest country
Russia
17 million sq km

Largest city
Tokyo 38 million

EUROPE

RUSSIA

St Petersburg
Moscow
Perm
Volgograd
Chelyabinsk
Omsk
Novosibirsk
Lake Baikal
Irkutsk
Yakutsk
Sea of Okhotsk
Sakhalin
Sapporo

Black Sea
Ankara
TURKEY
CYPRUS
LEBANON
ISRAEL
SYRIA
JORDAN
IRAQ
Baghdad
Tehran
KUWAIT
Kuwait
Riyadh
QATAR
BAHRAIN
UNITED ARAB EMIRATES
Muscat
SAUDI ARABIA
OMAN
Sanaa
YEMEN
Aden
Socotra (Yemen)

AFRICA
Red Sea
Tropic of Cancer

KAZAKHSTAN
Astana
Aral Sea
Lake Balkhash
Almaty
Ürümqi
Tashkent
UZBEKISTAN
TURKMENISTAN
Ashgabat
IRAN
Kabul
AFGHANISTAN
Islamabad
Lahore
PAKISTAN
Delhi
New Delhi
Karachi
NEPAL
BHUTAN
INDIA
BANGLADESH
Dhaka
Kolkata
Mumbai
Hyderabad
Chennai
Arabian Sea
Bay of Bengal
Andaman Is (India)
Nicobar Is (India)
SRI LANKA
Sri Jayewardenepura Kotte
Colombo
MALDIVES

MONGOLIA
Ulan Bator
Shenyang
Harbin
Beijing
Tianjin
Lanzhou
Xi'an
CHINA
Nanjing
Wuhan
Shanghai
Chongqing
Guangzhou
Hong Kong
PYONGYANG
NORTH KOREA
Seoul
SOUTH KOREA
Kobe
Osaka
Fukuoka
Sea of Japan (East Sea)
JAPAN
Tokyo
Taipei
TAIWAN

PACIFIC OCEAN

MYANMAR (BURMA)
Nay Pyi Taw
Yangon
Hanoi
Vientiane
LAOS
THAILAND
Bangkok
CAMBODIA
Phnom Penh
Ho Chi Minh City
VIETNAM
South China Sea
Luzon
PHILIPPINES
Manila
Mindanao
Davao
BRUNEI
MALAYSIA
Kuala Lumpur
Putrajaya
SINGAPORE
Borneo
Celebes
Makassar
INDONESIA
Sumatra
Jakarta
Java
Surabaya
Dili
EAST TIMOR (TIMOR-LESTE)

AUSTRALIA

INDIAN OCEAN

Arctic Circle
Equator
Tropic of Capricorn

N
W   E
S

Half the people in the world live in Asia, many of them in India and China.

Key to symbols

◢ Countries
■ Capital city
○ Important city/town

1 GEORGIA
2 ARMENIA
3 AZERBAIJAN
4 TAJIKISTAN
5 KYRGYZSTAN

500   1000   1500   2000   2500   3000 km

Scale : One centimetre on this map is the same as 500 kilometres on the ground.

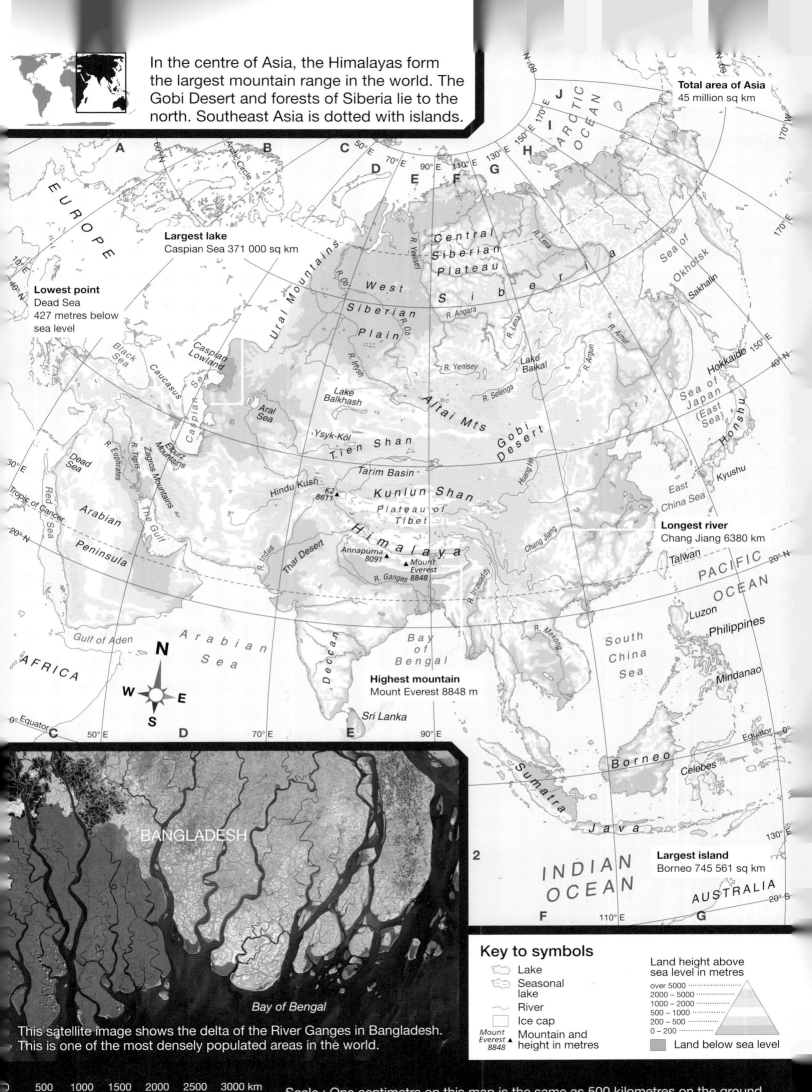

In the centre of Asia, the Himalayas form the largest mountain range in the world. The Gobi Desert and forests of Siberia lie to the north. Southeast Asia is dotted with islands.

Total area of Asia
45 million sq km

Largest lake
Caspian Sea 371 000 sq km

Lowest point
Dead Sea
427 metres below
sea level

Longest river
Chang Jiang 6380 km

Highest mountain
Mount Everest 8848 m

Largest island
Borneo 745 561 sq km

EUROPE

AFRICA

ARCTIC OCEAN

PACIFIC OCEAN

INDIAN OCEAN

AUSTRALIA

Arctic Circle
Tropic of Cancer
Equator

Ural Mountains
Central Siberian Plateau
West Siberian Plain
S i b e r i a
Sea of Okhotsk
Sakhalin
Caspian Lowland
Black Sea
Caucasus
Caspian Sea
Aral Sea
Lake Balkhash
R. Yenisey
R. Ob
R. Irtysh
R. Ob
R. Yenisey
R. Angara
R. Lena
R. Lena
R. Selenga
R. Amur
R. Argun
Hokkaido
Sea of Japan (East Sea)
Honshu
Kyushu
Altai Mts
Tien Shan
Ysyk-Köl
Gobi Desert
Elburz Mountains
Zagros Mountains
Dead Sea
R. Euphrates
R. Tigris
The Gulf
Red Sea
Gulf of Aden
Arabian Peninsula
Hindu Kush
K2 8611
Tarim Basin
Kunlun Shan
Plateau of Tibet
Himalaya
Annapurna 8091
Mount Everest 8848
R. Ganges
R. Indus
Thar Desert
Deccan
Arabian Sea
Bay of Bengal
Huang He
Chang Jiang
R. Irrawaddy
R. Mekong
East China Sea
South China Sea
Taiwan
Luzon
Philippines
Mindanao
Sri Lanka
Sumatra
Borneo
Java
Celebes

BANGLADESH

Bay of Bengal

This satellite image shows the delta of the River Ganges in Bangladesh. This is one of the most densely populated areas in the world.

Key to symbols

- Lake
- Seasonal lake
- River
- Ice cap
- Mount Everest ▲ 8848 — Mountain and height in metres

Land height above sea level in metres
- over 5000
- 2000 – 5000
- 1000 – 2000
- 500 – 1000
- 200 – 500
- 0 – 200

Land below sea level

500 1000 1500 2000 2500 3000 km

Scale : One centimetre on this map is the same as 500 kilometres on the ground

Africa, Asia and Europe join together in the Middle East. Many ancient civilisations grew up here. Today, the differences between people and religions have led to terrible conflicts.

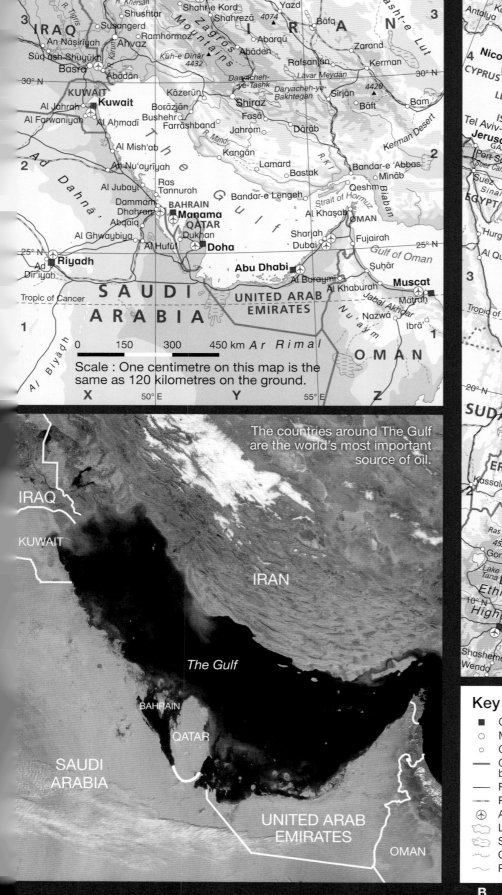

Scale : One centimetre on this map is the same as 120 kilometres on the ground.

0   150   300   450 km

The countries around The Gulf are the world's most important source of oil.

200   400   600   800   1000   1200 km

Key to symbols

■ Capital city
○ Main city/town
○ Other city/town
— Country boundary
— Road
–⊢ Railway
✈ Airport
Lake
Seasonal lake
Canal
River

☐ Ice cap

Mount Everest 8848 ▲ Mountain and height in metres

Land height above sea level in metres
over 5000
3000 – 5000
2000 – 3000
1000 – 2000
500 – 1000
200 – 500
0 – 200

Land below sea level

Scale : One centimetre on this map is the same as 200 kilometres on the ground.

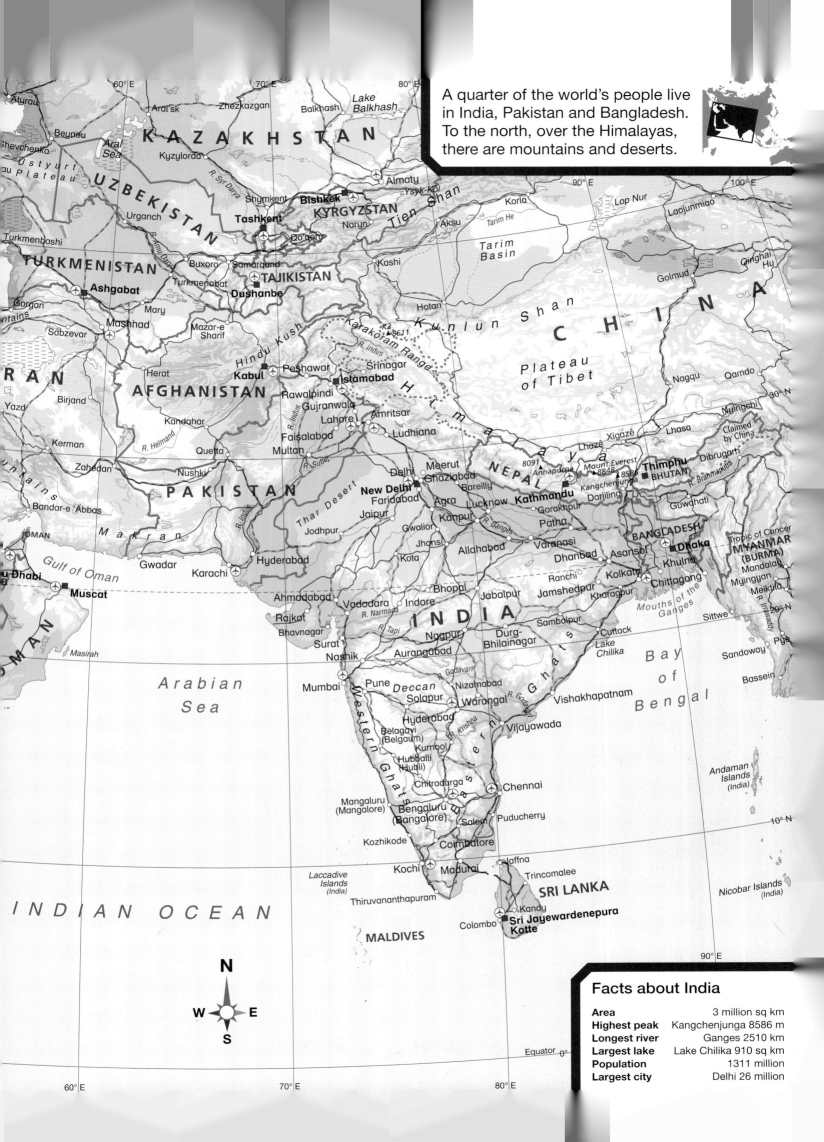

A quarter of the world's people live in India, Pakistan and Bangladesh. To the north, over the Himalayas, there are mountains and deserts.

Facts about India

Area	3 million sq km
Highest peak	Kangchenjunga 8586 m
Longest river	Ganges 2510 km
Largest lake	Lake Chilika 910 sq km
Population	1311 million
Largest city	Delhi 26 million

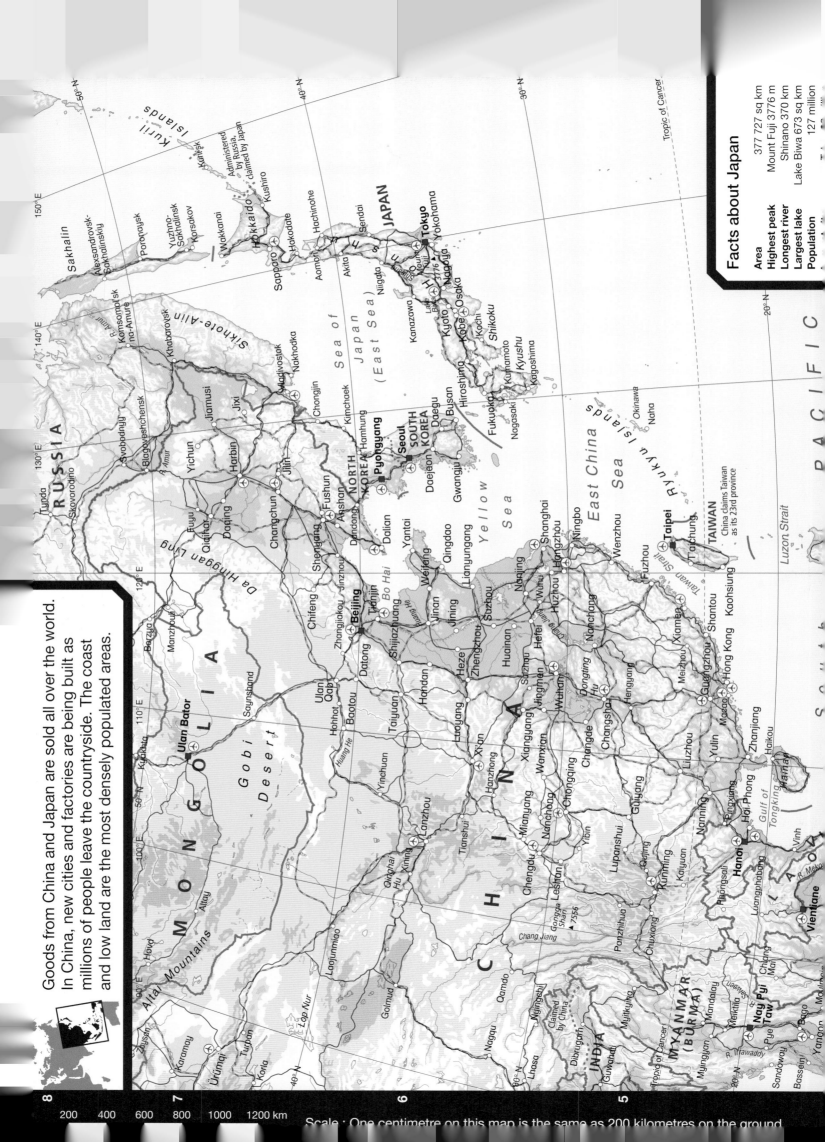

Goods from China and Japan are sold all over the world. In China, new cities and factories are being built as millions of people leave the countryside. The coast and low land are the most densely populated areas.

Facts about Japan

Area	377 727 sq km
Highest peak	Mount Fuji 3776 m
Longest river	Shinano 370 km
Largest lake	Lake Biwa 673 sq km
Population	127 million

RUSSIA

Sakhalin

Kuril Islands

Administered by Russia, claimed by Japan

HOKKAIDO

JAPAN

Tokyo
Yokohama
Nagoya
Kyoto
Kobe Osaka
Shikoku
Hiroshima
Kumamoto
Kyushu
Kagoshima
Fukuoka
Nagasaki

Sea of Japan (East Sea)

NORTH KOREA
Pyongyang
Hamhung

SOUTH KOREA
Seoul
Daejeon
Gwangju
Daegu
Busan

Yellow Sea

East China Sea

Ryukyu Islands
Okinawa
Naha

PACIFIC

TAIWAN
Taipei
Taichung
Kaohsiung
China claims Taiwan as its 23rd province

Luzon Strait
Taiwan Strait

MONGOLIA
Ulan Bator

Gobi Desert

Altai Mountains

CHINA

Beijing
Tianjin

Shanghai
Hong Kong
Guangzhou

Scale : One centimetre on this map is the same as 200 kilometres on the ground

200 400 600 800 1000 1200 km

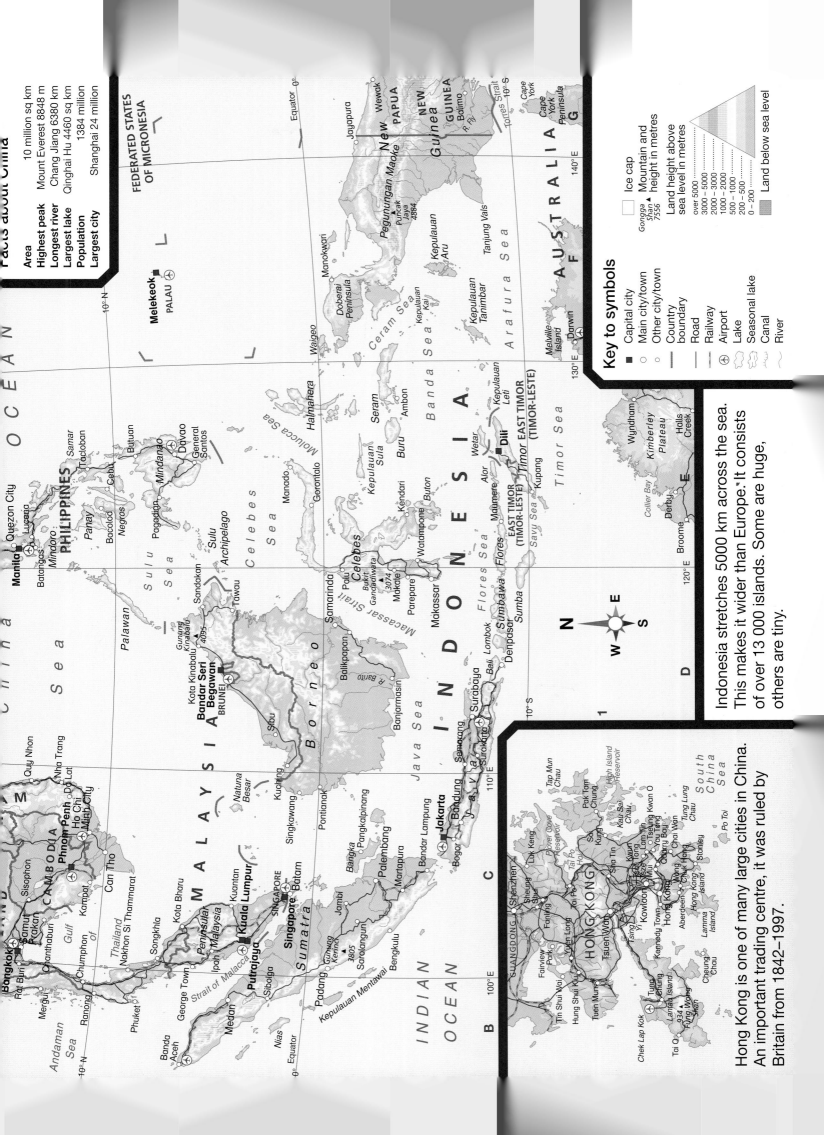

Facts about China

Area	10 million sq km
Highest peak	Mount Everest 8848 m
Longest river	Chang Jiang 6380 km
Largest lake	Qinghai Hu 4460 sq km
Population	1384 million
Largest city	Shanghai 24 million

Key to symbols

■ Capital city
○ Main city/town
○ Other city/town
— Country boundary
— Road
⊬⊬ Railway
✈ Airport
Lake
Seasonal lake
Canal
River

Ice cap
▲ Gongga Shan 7556 Mountain and height in metres

Land height above sea level in metres
over 5000
3000 – 5000
2000 – 3000
1000 – 2000
500 – 1000
200 – 500
0 – 200
Land below sea level

Indonesia stretches 5000 km across the sea. This makes it wider than Europe. It consists of over 13 000 islands. Some are huge, others are tiny.

Hong Kong is one of many large cities in China. An important trading centre, it was ruled by Britain from 1842–1997.

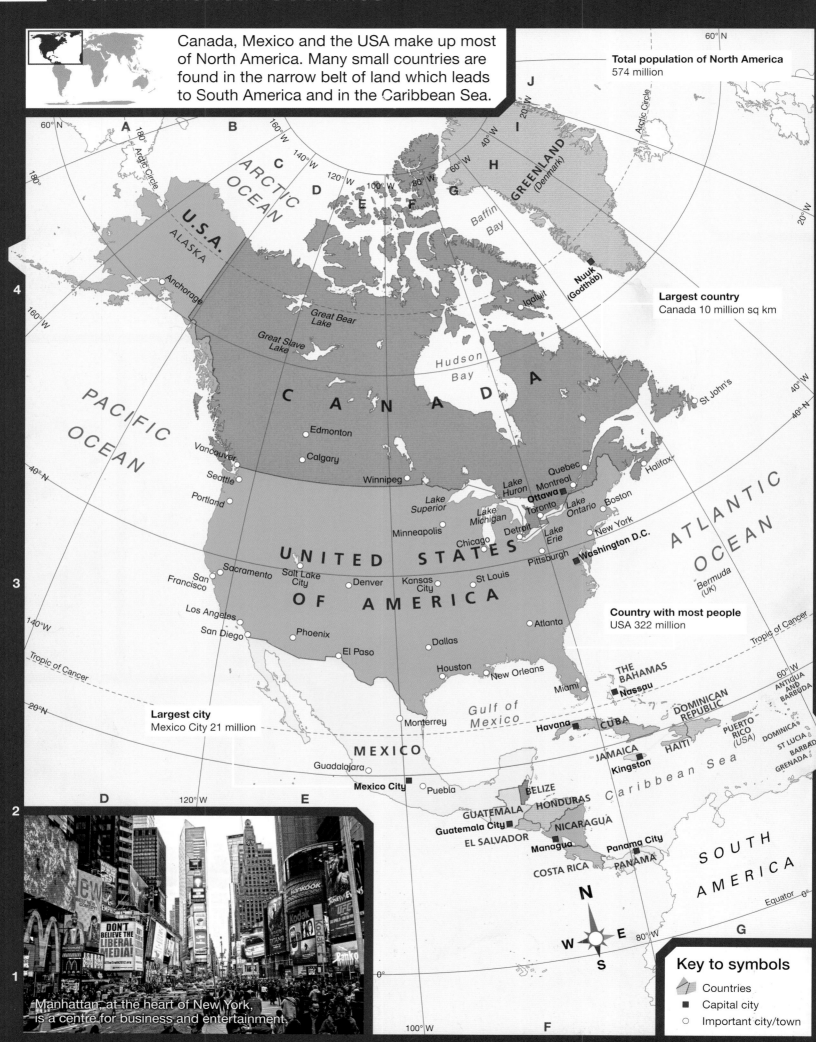

Canada, Mexico and the USA make up most of North America. Many small countries are found in the narrow belt of land which leads to South America and in the Caribbean Sea.

Total population of North America
574 million

Largest country
Canada 10 million sq km

Country with most people
USA 322 million

Largest city
Mexico City 21 million

ARCTIC OCEAN

GREENLAND (Denmark)

Baffin Bay

Nuuk (Godthåb)

Iqaluit

Great Bear Lake

Great Slave Lake

Hudson Bay

C A N A D A

St John's

PACIFIC OCEAN

Anchorage

U.S.A. ALASKA

Edmonton

Vancouver

Calgary

Seattle

Portland

Winnipeg

Lake Superior

Lake Huron

Lake Michigan

Quebec

Montreal

Ottawa

Toronto

Lake Ontario

Boston

Halifax

Minneapolis

Chicago

Detroit

Lake Erie

New York

ATLANTIC OCEAN

San Francisco

Sacramento

Salt Lake City

Denver

Kansas City

St Louis

Pittsburgh

Washington D.C.

UNITED STATES OF AMERICA

Bermuda (UK)

Los Angeles

San Diego

Phoenix

El Paso

Dallas

Atlanta

Houston

New Orleans

Miami

THE BAHAMAS

Nassau

Tropic of Cancer

ANTIGUA AND BARBUDA

Gulf of Mexico

Monterrey

Havana

CUBA

DOMINICAN REPUBLIC

PUERTO RICO (USA)

DOMINICA

Guadalajara

MEXICO

JAMAICA

HAITI

ST LUCIA

BARBADOS

GRENADA

Kingston

Caribbean Sea

Mexico City

Puebla

BELIZE

GUATEMALA

HONDURAS

Guatemala City

NICARAGUA

EL SALVADOR

Managua

Panama City

SOUTH AMERICA

COSTA RICA

PANAMA

Equator

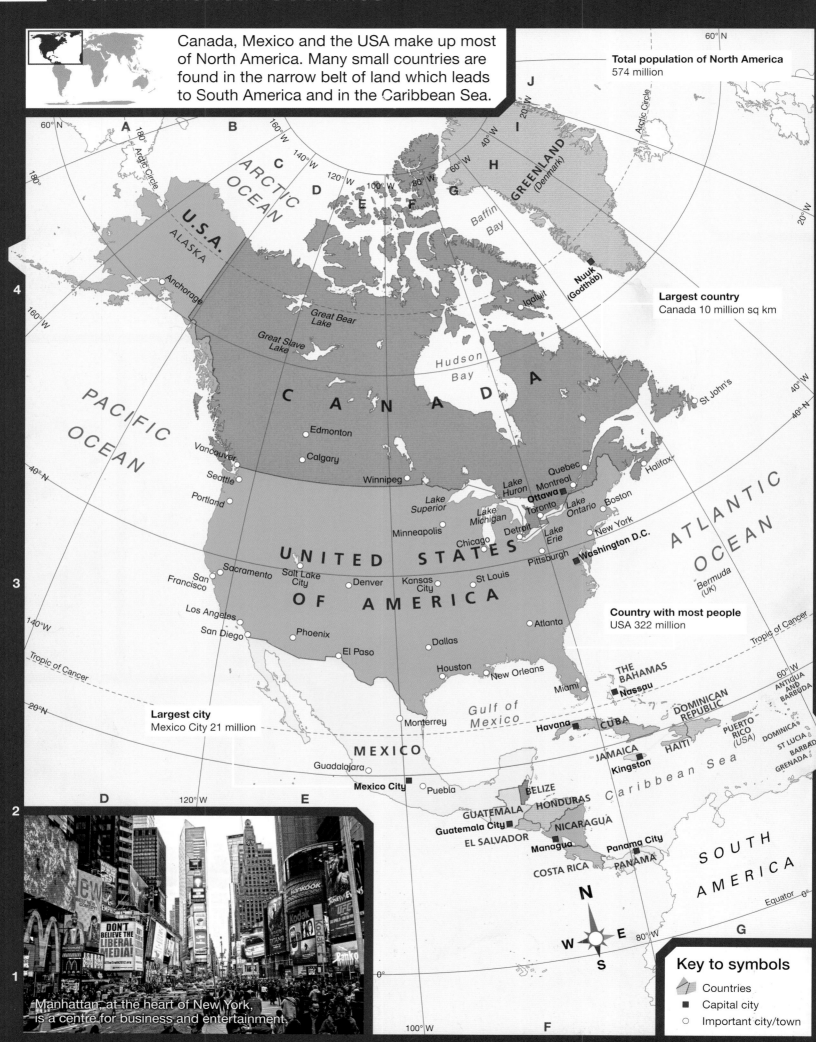
Manhattan, at the heart of New York, is a centre for business and entertainment.

Key to symbols
- ◢ Countries
- ■ Capital city
- ○ Important city/town

0 400 800 1200 1600 2000 km

Scale : One centimetre on this map is the same as 400 kilometres on the ground.

The Rocky Mountains stretch down the western side of North America. Further east there are lakes and plains. In the north, Greenland is covered in ice.

Total area of North America
25 million sq km

Largest island
Greenland 2 million sq km

Largest lake
Lake Superior 82 100 sq km

Highest mountain
Denali (Mount McKinley)
6190 m

Lowest point
Death Valley
86 metres below
sea level

Longest river
Mississippi-Missouri 5969 km

80° N   60° N

J   I   H   G   F   E   D   C   B   A

ARCTIC OCEAN

Arctic Circle

Ellesmere Island

Greenland

Baffin Bay

Baffin Island

Davis Strait

Cape Farewell

Victoria Island

R. Yukon

Denali (Mount McKinley) 6190 ▲

Mount Logan ▲ 5959

R. Mackenzie

Great Bear Lake

Great Slave Lake

Gulf of Alaska

Coast Mountains

R. Peace

Hudson Bay

Labrador

Newfoundland

PACIFIC OCEAN

Rocky Mountains

3954 ▲

Canadian Shield

R. St Lawrence

ATLANTIC OCEAN

Great Plains

Lake Superior

Great Lakes

Lake Huron

Lake Ontario

Cape Cod

Niagara Falls

Lake Michigan

Lake Erie

Appalachian Mountains

R. Snake

Great Salt Lake

Mount Elbert 4398

R. North Platte

R. Missouri

R. Ohio

▲ 2037

Great Basin

Death Valley Grand Canyon

Mount Whitney 4418 ▲

R. Colorado

R. Red

R. Mississippi

Tropic of Cancer

Gulf of California

Sierra Madre Occidental

Sierra Madre Oriental

Rio Grande

R. Brazos

Florida

20° N

Tropic of Cancer

Gulf of Mexico

Cuba

Hispaniola

Yucatán

Popocatépetl ▲ 5452

Caribbean Sea

Lake Nicaragua

Isthmus of Panama

SOUTH AMERICA

Equator

N W E S

Key to symbols

- ⬡ Lake
- ⬡ Seasonal lake
- ～ River
- ▢ Ice cap
- Denali 6190 ▲ Mountain and height in metres

Land height above sea level in metres

- over 5000
- 2000 – 5000
- 1000 – 2000
- 500 – 1000
- 200 – 500
- 0 – 200

▨ Land below sea level

The Grand Canyon on the Colorado River is 1500 metres deep and over 400 km long. It was one of the first National Parks in the USA.

0   400   800   1200   1600   2000 km

Scale : One centimetre on this map is the same as 400 kilometres on the ground.

180° 160° W 140° W 120° W 100° W 80° W 60° W 40° W 20° W

60° N 40° N 20° N

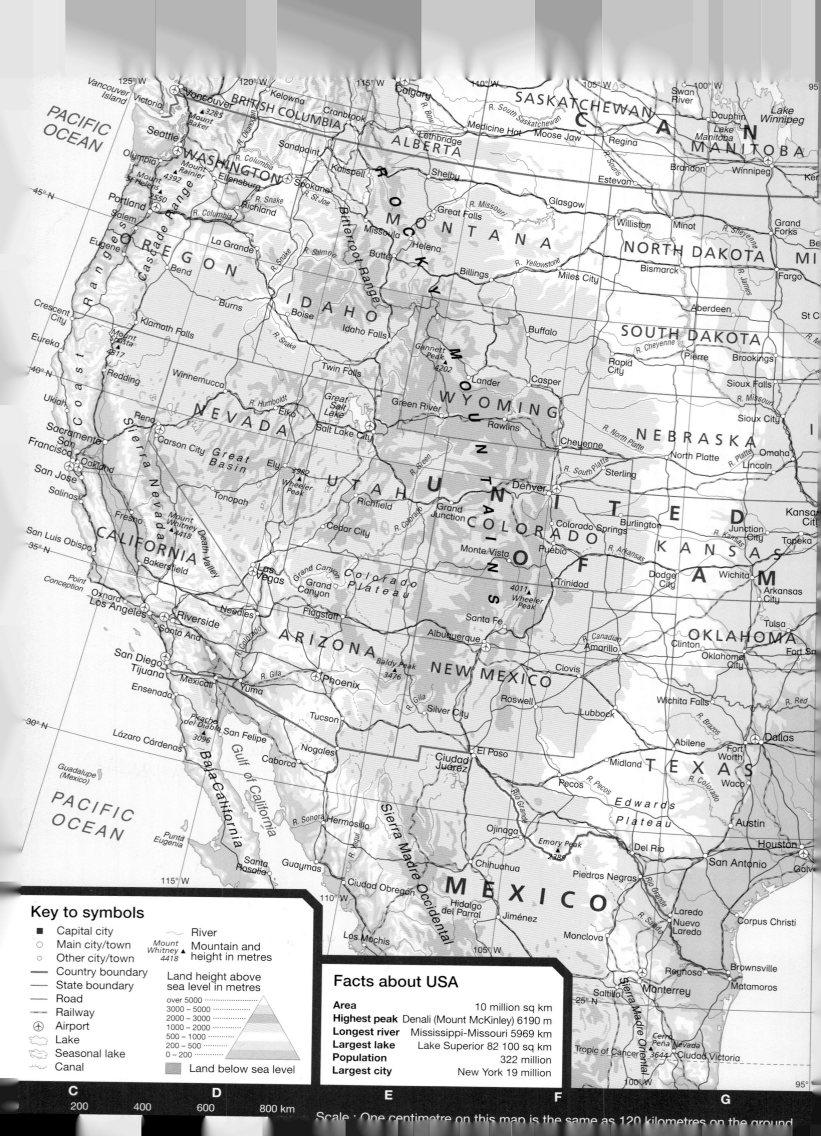

Key to symbols

- ■ Capital city
- ○ Main city/town
- ○ Other city/town
- —— Country boundary
- —— State boundary
- —— Road
- —— Railway
- ⊕ Airport
- Lake
- Seasonal lake
- Canal

~~ River

Mount
Whitney ▲ Mountain and
4418   height in metres

Land height above
sea level in metres

over 5000
3000 – 5000
2000 – 3000
1000 – 2000
500 – 1000
200 – 500
0 – 200

Land below sea level

Facts about USA

Area	10 million sq km
Highest peak	Denali (Mount McKinley) 6190 m
Longest river	Mississippi-Missouri 5969 km
Largest lake	Lake Superior 82 100 sq km
Population	322 million
Largest city	New York 19 million

Scale : One centimetre on this map is the same as 120 kilometres on the ground

200   400   600   800 km

There are 50 states in the USA. The smallest states are on the east coast, where settlers first arrived from Europe. Many states have straight boundaries that follow lines of latitude or longitude. Alaska and Hawaii are separated from the rest of the USA and are not shown on this map.

1 VERMONT
2 NEW HAMPSHIRE
3 MASSACHUSETTS
4 CONNECTICUT
5 RHODE ISLAND

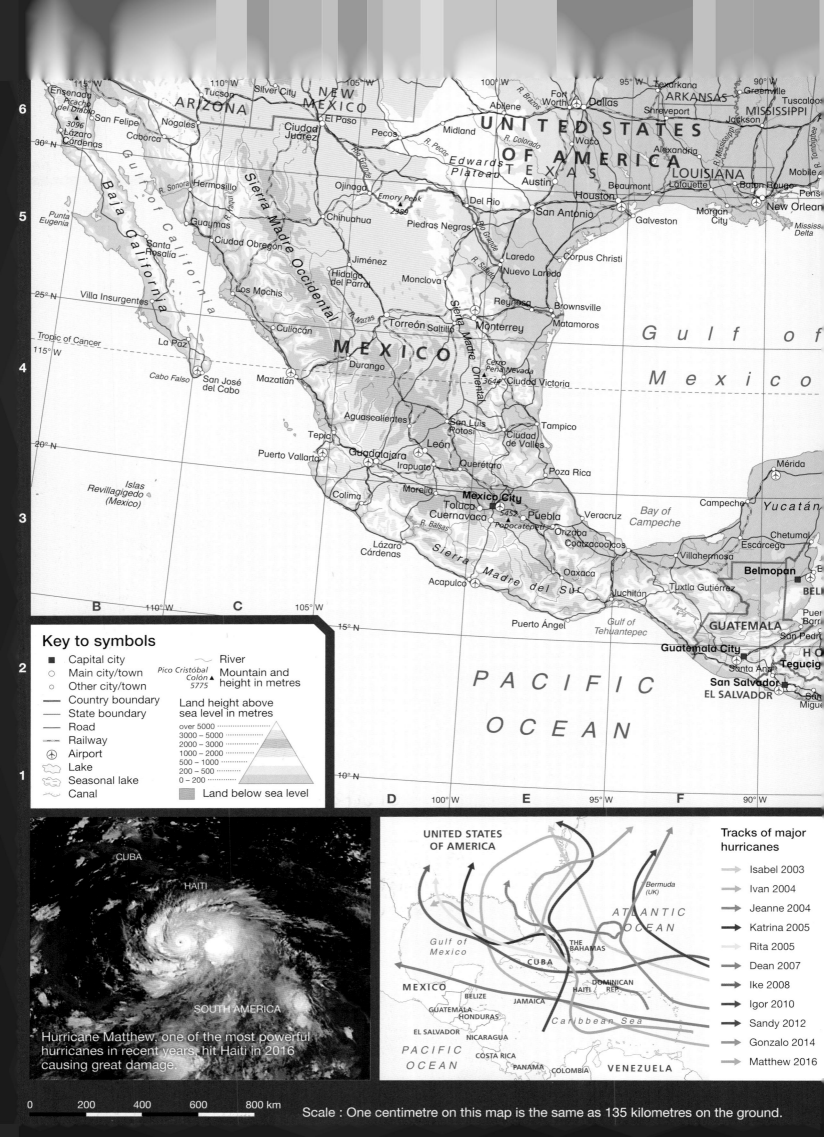

Key to symbols

- ■ Capital city
- ○ Main city/town
- ∘ Other city/town
- ── Country boundary
- ── State boundary
- ── Road
- ── Railway
- ⊕ Airport
- Lake
- Seasonal lake
- Canal

Pico Cristóbal Colón ▲ 5775

- ∿ River
- ▲ Mountain and height in metres

Land height above sea level in metres

- over 5000
- 3000 – 5000
- 2000 – 3000
- 1000 – 2000
- 500 – 1000
- 200 – 500
- 0 – 200

Land below sea level

Hurricane Matthew, one of the most powerful hurricanes in recent years, hit Haiti in 2016 causing great damage.

Tracks of major hurricanes

- → Isabel 2003
- → Ivan 2004
- → Jeanne 2004
- → Katrina 2005
- → Rita 2005
- → Dean 2007
- → Ike 2008
- → Igor 2010
- → Sandy 2012
- → Gonzalo 2014
- → Matthew 2016

0   200   400   600   800 km

Scale : One centimetre on this map is the same as 135 kilometres on the ground.

Mexico is eight times the size of the UK. With many high mountains, it has a population of over 120 million people. The Caribbean Sea to the east is dotted with islands. These are popular with tourists.

ATLANTIC OCEAN

N
W E
S

85° W · Atlanta
Augusta
ningham
Columbus
SOUTH CAROLINA
Charleston
ontgomery
80° W
75° W
GEORGIA
Savannah
Valdosta
nan
llahassee
Jacksonville
Lake City
Daytona Beach
30° N
FLORIDA
Cape Canaveral
70° W
65° W
60° W
Orlando
St Petersburg
Tampa
Lake Okeechobee
West Palm Beach
Fort Lauderdale
Miami
Florida Keys
Straits of Florida

Grand Bahama
Freeport City
Great Abaco
New Providence
Nassau
THE BAHAMAS
25° N
Tropic of Cancer

Andros
Cat Island
Great Exuma
Long Island

Havana
Matanzas
Pinar del Río
Guane
Santa Clara
CUBA
Camagüey
Holguín
Acklins Island
Turks and Caicos Islands (UK)
20° N

Cabo Antonio
ún
Isla de la Juventud
Bayamo
Guantánamo
Great Inagua
Grand Turk

Sa Maestra
Santiago de Cuba
Port-de-Paix
Cap-Haïtien
Santiago
Hispaniola
San Juan
Virgin Is (UK)
Leeward Islands
Anguilla (UK)
St-Martin (France)

Cayman Islands (UK)
Montego Bay
Jérémie
HAITI
Pico Duarte 3175
Santo Domingo
Ponce
PUERTO RICO (USA)
Virgin Is (USA)
Sint Maarten (Neth.)
Barbuda
ANTIGUA AND BARBUDA
St John's
Antigua

JAMAICA
Kingston
Port-au-Prince
DOMINICAN REPUBLIC
ST KITTS AND NEVIS
Montserrat (UK)
Guadeloupe (France)

Greater Antilles
Lesser Antilles
DOMINICA
Roseau
15° N
Martinique (France)

Caribbean
Castries
ST LUCIA
Windward Is

Sea
Kingstown
ST VINCENT AND THE GRENADINES
BARBADOS
Bridgetown

Lesser Antilles
GRENADA
St George's
TRINIDAD Tobago
AND TOBAGO

NICARAGUA
Rio Grande
Punta Gallinas
Aruba (Neth.)
Curaçao (Neth.)
Bonaire (Neth.)
Port of Spain
Cumaná
Güiria Trinidad
10° N

Managua
Lake aragua
Ríohacha
Coro
Caracas
Barcelona
Maturín
R. Tigre
Orinoco Delta

Barranquilla
Pico Cristóbal Colón 5775
Maracaibo
Barquisimeto
Valencia
Maracay
El Tigre
Ciudad Guayana

COSTA RICA
San José
Cartagena
Valledupar
Lake Maracaibo
Acarigua
Ciudad Bolívar
R. Orinoco

Chirripó 3819
Panama Canal
Colón
Sincelejo
Barinas
Embalse de Guri
El Callao

Isthmus of Panama
Panama City
Montería
R. Magdalena
San Fernando de Apure
VENEZUELA
5° N

David
Aguadulce
Turbo
Cúcuta
San Cristóbal

PANAMA
COLOMBIA
Bucaramanga
5493 Sierra Nevada del Cocuy
70° W
65° W

85° W
H
80° W
Medellín
Cúcuta
75° W
I
J
K
L

6
5
4
3
2
1

JAMAICA

Lucea
Montego Bay
Falmouth
St Ann's Bay
Oracabessa
Port Maria

Grange Hill
Cambridge
The Cockpit Country
Highgate
Annotto Bay

gril
Savanna-la-Mar
Christiana
Ewarton
Bog Walk
Blue Mt Peak 2256
Port Antonio

th West Point
Lacovia
Chapelton
Blue Mountains
Port Antonio

Black River
Mandeville
May Pen
Spanish Town
Kingston

Bull Savannah
Morant Bay
Port Morant

Portland Bight
Portland Point

TRINIDAD AND TOBAGO

VENEZUELA
Diego Martin
El Tucuche 936
Mt Aripo 940
Galera Point

Port of Spain
Tunapuna
Arima
Sangre Grande

Chaguanas
Gulf of Paria
Trinidad

Couva
Prince's Town
Rio Claro

San Fernando
Penal
Trinity Hills 304
Galeota Point

Point Fortin
Siparia

ST LUCIA

Pointe du Cap
Cap Marquis

Castries

Anse-la-Raye
Dennery

Mount Gimie 950
Soufrière
Micoud

Choiseul
Laborie
Vieux Fort

A   B   C   D

5

Brazil covers nearly half of South America. Argentina and Peru are also large countries. Chile is 4000 km long but only a few hundred kilometres wide.

Tropic of Cancer   40° W

Total population of South America
418 million

20° N   20° N

NORTH AMERICA

Caribbean Sea

4

80° W   60° W

Barranquilla   Maracaibo   Caracas   Port of Spain
TRINIDAD AND TOBAGO

VENEZUELA

Medellín   Georgetown
Paramaribo
GUYANA   Cayenne
SURINAME
FRENCH GUIANA

Bogotá
Cali   **COLOMBIA**

N
W   E
S

Quito
ECUADOR
Guayaquil   Belém   Equator   0°

Equator   0°
Galapagos Islands (Ecuador)   São Luís
Iquitos   Manaus   Fortaleza

Trujillo   Natal

PERU   B R A Z I L   Recife

3

Largest country
Brazil 9 million sq km

Lima   Aracaju
Salvador

Lake Titicaca   **Brasília**

BOLIVIA   **Largest city**
São Paulo 21 million

Country with most people
Brazil 208 million

Arequipa   **La Paz**

Sucre   Belo Horizonte

Antofagasta   **PARAGUAY**   São Paulo   Rio de Janeiro   20° S

20° S   **Asunción**   Tropic of Capricorn
Tropic of Capricorn   Curitiba

A T L A N T I C

O C E A N

C
H
I
L
E
Valparaíso   Porto Alegre

2

Juan Fernandez Islands (Chile)   **URUGUAY**

Santiago   **Buenos Aires**   Montevideo

Concepción   A
R
G
E
N
T
I
N
A   Mar del Plata
40° S   40° W   D   20° W

P A C I F I C

O C E A N

40° S

Falkland Islands (UK)
Claimed by Argentina

Punta Arenas

1

60° S

60° S

Antarctic Circle

Key to symbols
- ◤ Countries
- ■ Capital city
- ○ Important city/town

100° W   A   80° W   B   60° W   C

Rio de Janeiro is a huge city built around one of the best natural harbours in South America.

0   400   800   1200   1600   2000 km

Scale : One centimetre on this map is the same as 400 kilometres on the ground.

The Andes, which run down the western edge of South America, are the world's longest chain of mountains. From here the river Amazon flows east to the Atlantic Ocean.

Total area of South America
18 million sq km

Longest river
River Amazon 6516 km

Largest lake
Lake Titicaca 8340 sq km

Highest mountain
Aconcagua 6959 m

Lowest point
Laguna del Carbon 105 m below sea level

Largest island
Tierra del Fuego 47 000 sq km

100° W
80° W
60° W
40° W
20° W

Tropic of Cancer
20° N
Equator 0°
20° S
Tropic of Capricorn
40° S

NORTH AMERICA

Caribbean Sea

N
W E
S

Lake Maracaibo
Orinoco Delta
R. Orinoco
Llanos
Angel Falls
Mount Roraima 2810
Guiana Highlands
Mouths of the Amazon

Galapagos Islands

R. Japurá
R. Negro
R. Amazon
Amazon Basin
R. Amazon
Selvas
R. Purus
R. Madeira
R. Tocantins
R. São Francisco

Lake Titicaca
Andes
Atacama Desert
Altiplano

Brazilian Highlands

Gran Chaco
R. Paraguay
Nevado Ojos del Salado 6908
R. Salado
R. Paraná
R. Uruguay

ATLANTIC OCEAN

Aconcagua 6959
Pampas
Rio de la Plata

Juan Fernandez Islands

PACIFIC OCEAN

R. Colorado
R. Negro

Isla de Chiloé
Patagonia
Valdes Peninsula

Falkland Islands

Tierra del Fuego
Cape Horn

South Georgia

Key to symbols
- Lake
- Seasonal lake
- River
- *Aconcagua* 6959 ▲ Mountain and height in metres

Land height above sea level in metres

over 5000	
2000 – 5000	
1000 – 2000	
500 – 1000	
200 – 500	
0 – 200	

Land below sea level

In South America large areas of rainforest have been cleared for farming, such as the soy plantation in this photo.

0 400 800 1200 1600 2000 km

Scale : One centimetre on this map is the same as 400 kilometres on the ground.

In South America many people live in towns and cities. The coast is the most crowded. The mountains and other inland areas are much emptier.

N · E · S · W

ATLANTIC OCEAN

Caribbean Sea

Lesser Antilles

DOMINICA
MARTINIQUE (Fr.)
ST LUCIA
BARBADOS
ST VINCENT AND THE GRENADINES
GRENADA
TRINIDAD AND TOBAGO
Port of Spain

Aruba (Neth.)
Curaçao (Neth.)

NICARAGUA
COSTA RICA
PANAMA
Panama City

Barranquilla
Cartagena
Monteria
Sincelejo
Pico Cristóbal Colón ▲5775
Maracaibo
Lake Maracaibo
San Cristóbal
Bucaramanga
Medellín
Manizales
Cali
Pasto
Quito
ECUADOR
Cotopaxi 5896 ▲
Ambato
Portoviejo
Guayaquil
Machala
Piura
Chiclayo
Trujillo
Chimbote
Huascarán 6768 ▲
Lima
Callao
Ayacucho
Cusco
Arequipa
Coropuna 6425 ▲
Arica
Iquique

COLOMBIA
Bogotá
Villavicencio
Florencia

VENEZUELA
Caracas
Valencia
Maracay
Barcelona
Barquisimeto
Coro
Güiria
Maturín
Ciudad Bolívar
Ciudad Guayana
Barinas
Acarigua
San Fernando de Apure

R. Orinoco
Orinoco Delta
R. Apure
R. Meta
R. Guaviare
R. Magdalena

GUYANA
Georgetown
SURINAME
Paramaribo
FRENCH GUIANA
Cayenne

Claimed by Venezuela
Claimed by Suriname
Claimed by Suriname

R. Essequibo
Mount Roraima 2810 ▲
Pico da Neblina 3014 ▲
Guiana Highlands

Llanos Oriental

PERU
Cruzeiro do Sul
Pucallpa
Huancayo
Juliaca
Cordillera Occidental
Cordillera Central
Cordillera Oriental
ANDES
Cordillera Occidental
Cord. Occidental
Altiplano
Sajama 6542 ▲
Lake Titicaca
La Paz
Cochabamba
Sucre
Potosí
Tarija

BOLIVIA
Santa Cruz
Trinidad

R. Marañón
R. Ucayali
R. Yavari
R. Putumayo
R. Caquetá
R. Japurá
R. Juruá
R. Purus
R. Madre de Dios
R. Beni
R. Mamoré
R. Guaporé
R. San Miguel
R. Paraguay
R. Taquari

BRAZIL
Brasília
Manaus
Macapurú
Manacapuru
Boa Vista
R. Branco
R. Negro
R. Amazon
R. Madeira
R. Juruena
R. Teles Pires
R. Theodore Roosevelt
R. Iparaná
Porto Velho
Ariquemes
Rio Branco

Amazon Basin
Selvas

Mouths of the Amazon
Ilha de Marajó
Belém
Bragança
São Luís
Bacabal
Imperatriz
Araguaína
Marabá
Altamira
Itaituba
R. Tapajós
R. Iriri
R. Xingu
R. Tocantins
R. Araguaia
Tucuruí Resr.
Balbina Resr.

Parnaíba
Sobral
Fortaleza
Teresina
R. Parnaíba
Natal
Recife
Caruaru
Garanhuns
Maceió
Aracaju
Salvador
Itabuna
Feira de Santana
Paulo Afonso
Petrolina
Sobradinho Dam
R. São Francisco
Serra da Mesa Resr.
Brazilian Highlands
Serra do Mar
Montes Claros
Itambé 2033 ▲
Teófilo Otôni
Governador Valadares
Linhares
Vitória
Belo Horizonte
Barbacena
Araçatuba
Araraquara
Barretos
Campo Grande
Rio Verde
Goiânia
Anápolis
Luziânia
Uberlândia
Uberaba
Cáceres
Corumbá
Cuiabá
Rondonópolis

Equator
0°
10° N
10° S
20° S
80° W
70° W
60° W
50° W
40° W

Scale: One centimetre on this map is the same as 200 kilometres on the ground.

0   200   400   600   800   1000   1200 km

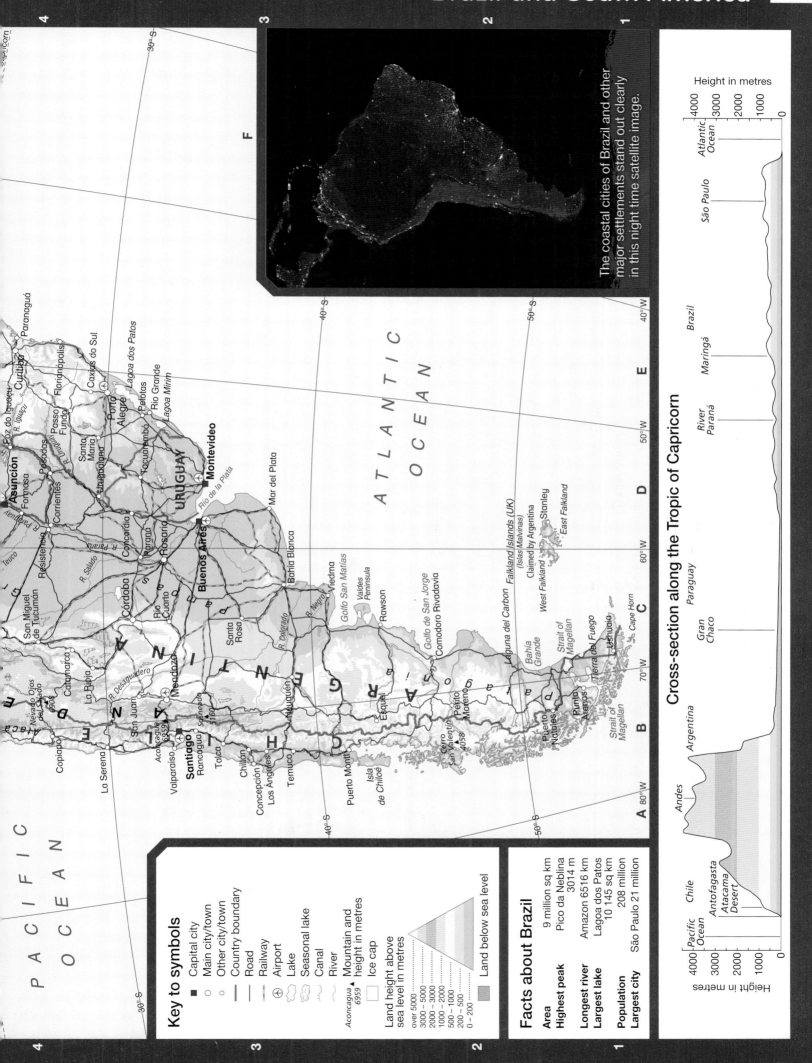

Key to symbols

- ■ Capital city
- ○ Main city/town
- ○ Other city/town
- Country boundary
- Road
- Railway
- ✈ Airport
- Lake
- Seasonal lake
- Canal
- River
- ▲ Mountain and height in metres
  Aconcagua 6959
- Ice cap

Land height above sea level in metres

- over 5000
- 3000 – 5000
- 2000 – 3000
- 1000 – 2000
- 500 – 1000
- 200 – 500
- 0 – 200

Land below sea level

Facts about Brazil

Area	9 million sq km
Highest peak	Pico da Neblina 3014 m
Longest river	Amazon 6516 km
Largest lake	Lagoa dos Patos 10 145 sq km
Population	208 million
Largest city	São Paulo 21 million

The coastal cities of Brazil and other major settlements stand out clearly in this night time satellite image.

Cross-section along the Tropic of Capricorn

Height in metres

Pacific Ocean — Chile — Antofagasta — Atacama Desert — Andes — Argentina — Gran Chaco — Paraguay — River Paraná — Maringá — Brazil — São Paulo — Atlantic Ocean

4000 3000 2000 1000 0

A   B   C   D   E   F   G

Australia, New Zealand and Papua New Guinea are the largest countries in Oceania. Other countries are made up of groups of islands scattered across the Pacific Ocean.

Total population of Oceania
39 million

160° E   170° E

N
W   E
S

Equator

Yaren
NAURU

KIRIBATI

120° E   130° E   140° E   150° E

Equator   0°

ASIA

New Guinea

PAPUA
NEW GUINEA

Lae

SOLOMON
ISLANDS

TUVALU

Arafura Sea

10° S

**Port
Moresby**

Honiara

10° S

Timor Sea

Darwin

Coral Sea

VANUATU

INDIAN
OCEAN

Cairns

Port Vila

Townsville

FIJI

New
Caledonia
(France)

Nouméa

Rockhampton

20° S

20° S

Alice
Springs

Tropic of Capricorn

Largest country
Australia 8 million sq km

Tropic of Capricorn

A U S T R A L I A

PACIFIC
OCEAN

Brisbane
Gold Coast

Kati Thanda-
Lake Eyre

Kalgoorlie

Newcastle

Country with most people
Australia 24 million

30° S

30° S

Great
Australian Bight

Sydney

Perth

Adelaide

Canberra

Melbourne

Tasman Sea

North
Island

Auckland

Geelong

NEW
ZEALAND

Tasmania

Wellington

110° E   A   120° E

Hobart

Christchurch

South
Island

40° S

Dunedin

Largest city
Sydney 5 million

International Date Line

B   130° E   C   140° E   D   150° E   E   160° E   F   170° E   G   180°   H   170° W

Key to symbols

Countries

■ Capital city

○ Important city/town

Tuvalu is made up of a chain of nine small islands and coral reefs. There are only 12 000 people in the whole country.

0   300   600   900   1200   1500   1800   2100 km

Scale : One centimetre on this map is the same as 325 kilometres on the ground.

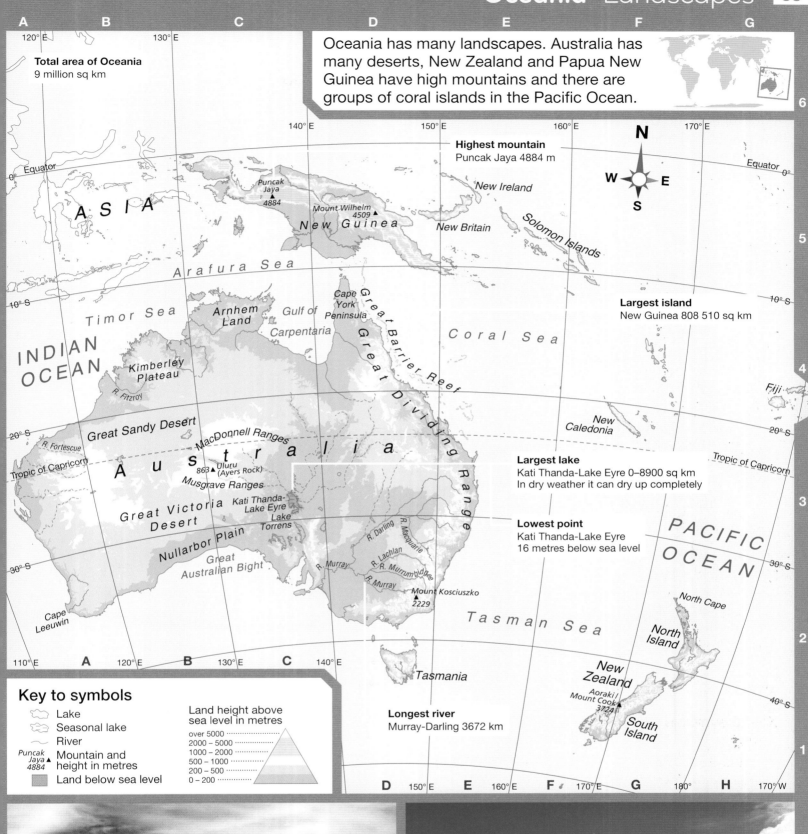

Oceania has many landscapes. Australia has many deserts, New Zealand and Papua New Guinea have high mountains and there are groups of coral islands in the Pacific Ocean.

Total area of Oceania
9 million sq km

Highest mountain
Puncak Jaya 4884 m

Largest island
New Guinea 808 510 sq km

Largest lake
Kati Thanda-Lake Eyre 0–8900 sq km
In dry weather it can dry up completely

Lowest point
Kati Thanda-Lake Eyre
16 metres below sea level

Longest river
Murray-Darling 3672 km

A S I A

New Guinea

Puncak Jaya 4884

Mount Wilhelm 4509 ▲

New Ireland

New Britain

Solomon Islands

Arafura Sea

Timor Sea

Arnhem Land

Gulf of Carpentaria

Cape York Peninsula

Great Barrier Reef

Coral Sea

INDIAN OCEAN

Kimberley Plateau

R. Fitzroy

Great Sandy Desert

R. Fortescue

MacDonnell Ranges

Australia

863 ▲ Uluru (Ayers Rock)

Musgrave Ranges

Great Victoria Desert

Kati Thanda-Lake Eyre

Lake Torrens

Nullarbor Plain

Great Australian Bight

R. Darling

R. Macquarie

R. Lachlan

R. Murrumbidgee

R. Murray

R. Murray

Great Dividing Range

Mount Kosciuszko 2229 ▲

Tropic of Capricorn

Cape Leeuwin

Tasman Sea

Tasmania

PACIFIC OCEAN

New Caledonia

Fiji

North Cape

North Island

New Zealand

Aoraki / Mount Cook 3724

South Island

Key to symbols

〜 Lake
〜 Seasonal lake
〜 River
Puncak Jaya 4884 ▲ Mountain and height in metres
▨ Land below sea level

Land height above sea level in metres
over 5000
2000 – 5000
1000 – 2000
500 – 1000
200 – 500
0 – 200

Uluru (Ayers Rock) in the middle of Australia is a World Heritage site and a holy place for Aborigines.

Aoraki / Mount Cook is the highest mountain in New Zealand. The name means 'cloud piercer' in the local language.

0   300   600   900   1200   1500   1800   2100 km

Scale : One centimetre on this map is the same as 325 kilometres on the ground.

Antarctica is the world's coldest, driest and windiest continent. It is covered by a thick sheet of ice. In many places the ice is thicker than the highest mountains in the UK. Very few plants and animals survive here.

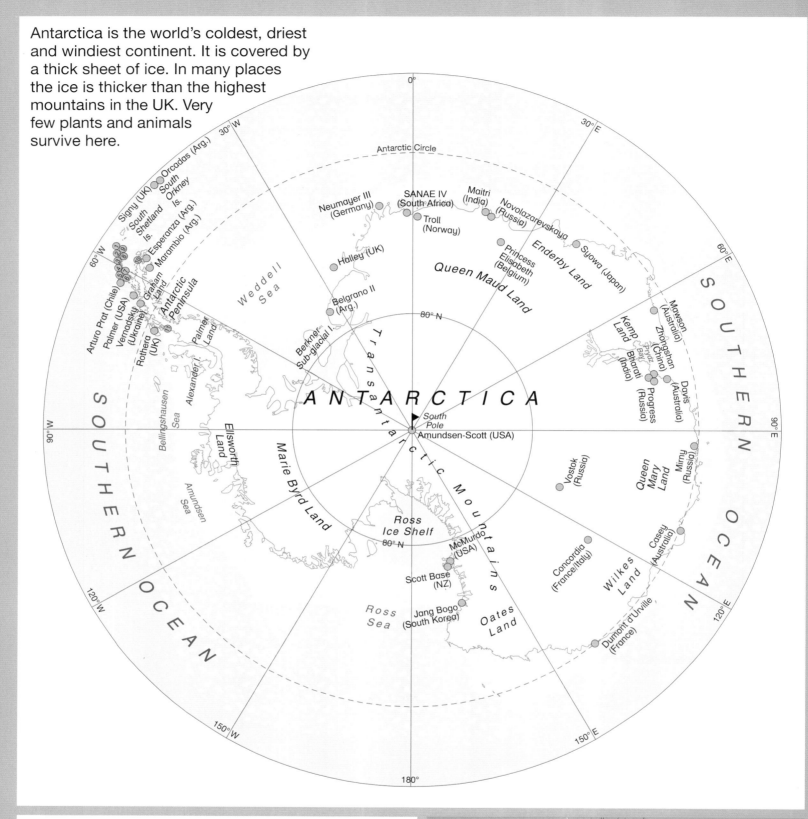

Key to symbols

- ☐ Ice shelf
- ☐ Ice cap
- ☐ Polar pack ice
- ☐ Drifting ice
- ⬤ Manned bases

Names of bases numbered on map

① Comandante Ferraz (Brazil)
② King Sejong (South Korea)
③ Artigas (Uruguay)
④ Frei (Chile)
⑤ Bellingshausen (Russia)
⑥ Great Wall (China)
⑦ Escudero (Chile)
⑧ Carlini (Argentina)
⑨ Arctowski (Poland)
⑩ Bernardo O'Higgins (Chile)
⑪ San Martin (Argentina)

There has been an American research station at the South Pole for the past 60 years.

| 0 | 500 | 1000 | 1500 | 2000 km |

Scale : One centimetre on this map is the same as 350 kilometres on the ground.

The Arctic Ocean is the smallest of the world's oceans. It is very cold and mostly covered with sea ice. In summer whales, seals and other creatures come to the Arctic Ocean looking for food.

The people who live in the Arctic are known as the Inuit. They still sometimes travel by dog sleigh.

Key to symbols

- Lake
- River
- Ice cap
- Polar pack ice
- Drifting ice

Land height above sea level in metres

| over 2000 |
| 1000 – 2000 |
| 500 – 1000 |
| 200 – 500 |
| 0 – 200 |

Scale : One centimetre on this map is the same as 350 kilometres on the ground.

0   500   1000   1500   2000 km

There are nearly 200 countries in the world. Russia is the largest, China has the most people and Monaco (Europe) is the most crowded.

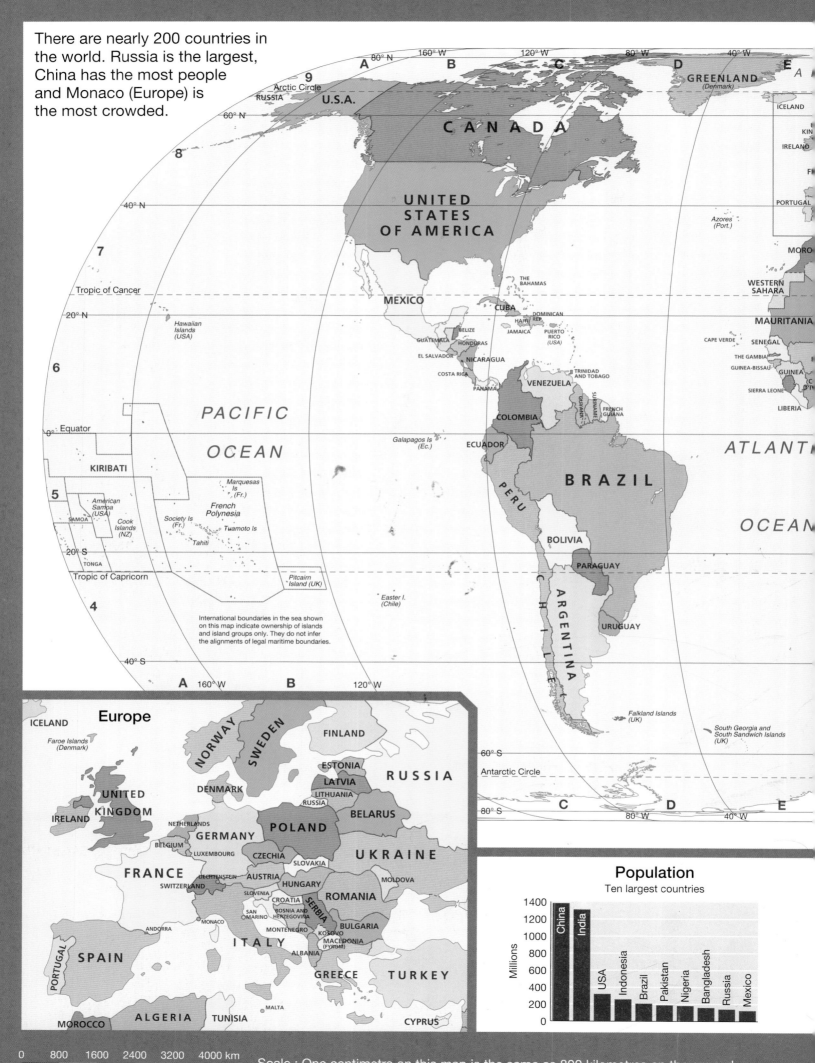

80° N   160° W   120° W   80° W   40° W

A   B   C   D   E

9   Arctic Circle
RUSSIA   U.S.A.   GREENLAND
(Denmark)
ICELAND
60° N   CANADA   KIN
8   IRELAND
FI
40° N   UNITED
STATES
OF AMERICA   PORTUGAL
7   Azores
(Port.)
MORO
Tropic of Cancer   MEXICO   WESTERN
SAHARA
20° N   CUBA   DOMINICAN
BELIZE   HAITI   REP.   MAURITANIA
THE BAHAMAS   JAMAICA   PUERTO RICO (USA)   CAPE VERDE   SENEGAL
6   GUATEMALA   HONDURAS   THE GAMBIA
EL SALVADOR   NICARAGUA   GUINEA-BISSAU   GUINEA
COSTA RICA   TRINIDAD AND TOBAGO   SIERRA LEONE   C D'IV
PANAMA   VENEZUELA   LIBERIA
COLOMBIA   GUYANA   SURINAME   FRENCH GUIANA
Galapagos Is
0° Equator   (Ec.)   ECUADOR   ATLANT
PACIFIC   PERU   BRAZIL
OCEAN   OCEAN
KIRIBATI
Marquesas
Is (Fr.)   BOLIVIA
5   American
Samoa   French
Polynesia
(USA)   Society Is   Tuamoto Is   PARAGUAY
SAMOA   (Fr.)
Cook   Tahiti   ARGENTINA
Islands
(NZ)   URUGUAY
20° S   TONGA
Tropic of Capricorn   Pitcairn
Island (UK)
4   Easter I.
(Chile)   CHILE

International boundaries in the sea shown on this map indicate ownership of islands and island groups only. They do not infer the alignments of legal maritime boundaries.

40° S

A   160° W   B   120° W

Falkland Islands
(UK)
South Georgia and
South Sandwich Islands
(UK)
60° S
Antarctic Circle
80° S   80° W   40° W
C   D   E

Europe

ICELAND
Faroe Islands
(Denmark)   NORWAY   SWEDEN   FINLAND
ESTONIA
DENMARK   LATVIA
LITHUANIA
RUSSIA
UNITED   BELARUS
KINGDOM
NETHERLANDS   POLAND
IRELAND   GERMANY   UKRAINE
BELGIUM   CZECHIA   SLOVAKIA
LUXEMBOURG   MOLDOVA
FRANCE   LIECHTENSTEIN   AUSTRIA   HUNGARY
SWITZERLAND   SLOVENIA   ROMANIA
CROATIA   SERBIA
SAN   BOSNIA AND
MARINO   HERZEGOVINA
ANDORRA   MONACO   MONTENEGRO   BULGARIA
KOSOVO
ITALY   MACEDONIA
(FYROM)
ALBANIA
PORTUGAL   SPAIN   GREECE   TURKEY
MALTA
MOROCCO   ALGERIA   TUNISIA   CYPRUS

Population
Ten largest countries

<!-- Bar chart: Millions on y-axis from 0 to 1400 -->

China	~1400
India	~1300
USA	~300
Indonesia	~250
Brazil	~200
Pakistan	~200
Nigeria	~180
Bangladesh	~160
Russia	~140
Mexico	~130

0   800   1600   2400   3200   4000 km

Scale : One centimetre on this map is the same as 800 kilometres on the ground.

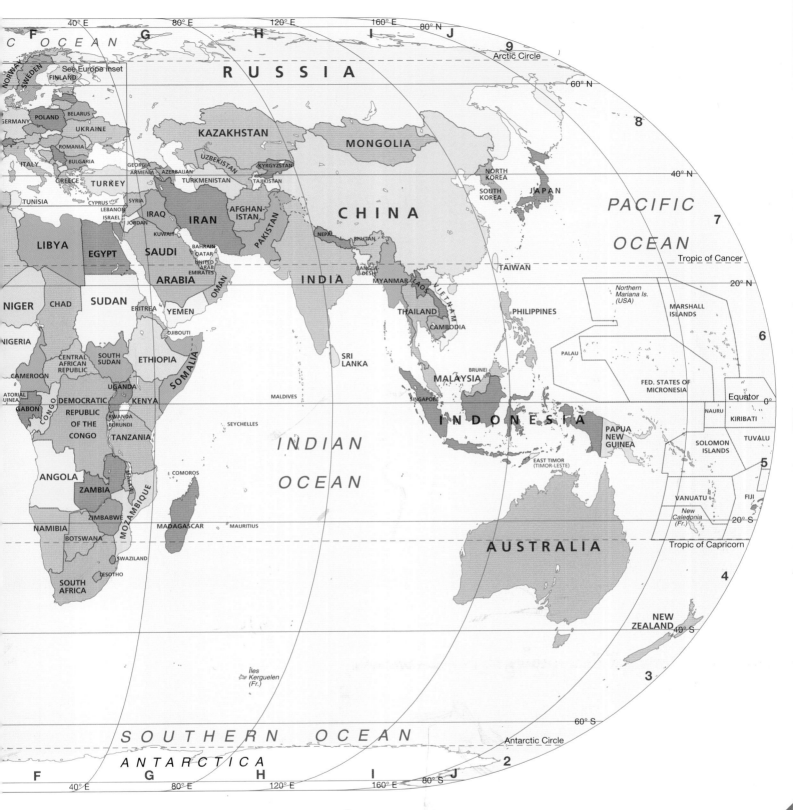

RUSSIA

C OCEAN

NORWAY
SWEDEN
FINLAND
See Europe inset
GERMANY
POLAND
BELARUS
UKRAINE
ROMANIA
ITALY
BULGARIA
GREECE
TURKEY
TUNISIA
CYPRUS
LEBANON
SYRIA
ISRAEL
JORDAN
IRAQ
KUWAIT

GEORGIA
ARMENIA
AZERBAIJAN

KAZAKHSTAN

UZBEKISTAN
TURKMENISTAN
KYRGYZSTAN
TAJIKISTAN

MONGOLIA

IRAN
AFGHAN-
ISTAN
PAKISTAN

CHINA

NORTH
KOREA
SOUTH
KOREA
JAPAN

PACIFIC

OCEAN

LIBYA
EGYPT
SAUDI
ARABIA

BAHRAIN
QATAR
UNITED
ARAB
EMIRATES
OMAN

NEPAL
BHUTAN
INDIA
BANGLA-
DESH
MYANMAR
LAOS
VIETNAM

TAIWAN

Tropic of Cancer

Northern
Mariana Is.
(USA)

MARSHALL
ISLANDS

NIGER
CHAD
SUDAN
ERITREA
YEMEN
DJIBOUTI

THAILAND
CAMBODIA

PHILIPPINES

NIGERIA

CENTRAL
AFRICAN
REPUBLIC
SOUTH
SUDAN
ETHIOPIA
SOMALIA

SRI
LANKA

MALAYSIA
BRUNEI

PALAU

FED. STATES OF
MICRONESIA

CAMEROON
ATORIAL
UINEA
GABON
CONGO
DEMOCRATIC
REPUBLIC
OF THE
CONGO
UGANDA
KENYA
RWANDA
BURUNDI
TANZANIA

MALDIVES

SEYCHELLES

SINGAPORE

INDONESIA

Equator

NAURU
KIRIBATI

PAPUA
NEW
GUINEA

SOLOMON
ISLANDS

TUVALU

ANGOLA
ZAMBIA
MOZAMBIQUE
ZIMBABWE

COMOROS

MADAGASCAR
MAURITIUS

INDIAN

OCEAN

EAST TIMOR
(TIMOR-LESTE)

VANUATU
New
Caledonia
(Fr.)

FIJI

NAMIBIA
BOTSWANA
SWAZILAND
LESOTHO
SOUTH
AFRICA

Îles
Kerguelen
(Fr.)

AUSTRALIA

NEW
ZEALAND

SOUTHERN   OCEAN

Antarctic Circle

ANTARCTICA

Arctic Circle
60° N
40° N
20° N
Equator 0°
20° S
Tropic of Capricorn
40° S
60° S

40° E   80° E   120° E   160° E   80° N

9
8
7
6
5
4
3
2

C   G   H   I   J
F   G   H   I   J
40° E   80° E   120° E   160° E   80° S

Number of countries

Number of countries in the world

200
160
120
80
40
0

1950
2017

Total world population
7349 million

Largest country
Russia 17 million sq km

Country with most people
China 1384 million

World's newest country
South Sudan (2011)

Land area
Ten largest countries

Million square kilometres

18
16
14
12
10
8
6
4
2
0

Russia
Canada
USA
China
Brazil
Australia
India
Argentina
Kazakhstan
Algeria

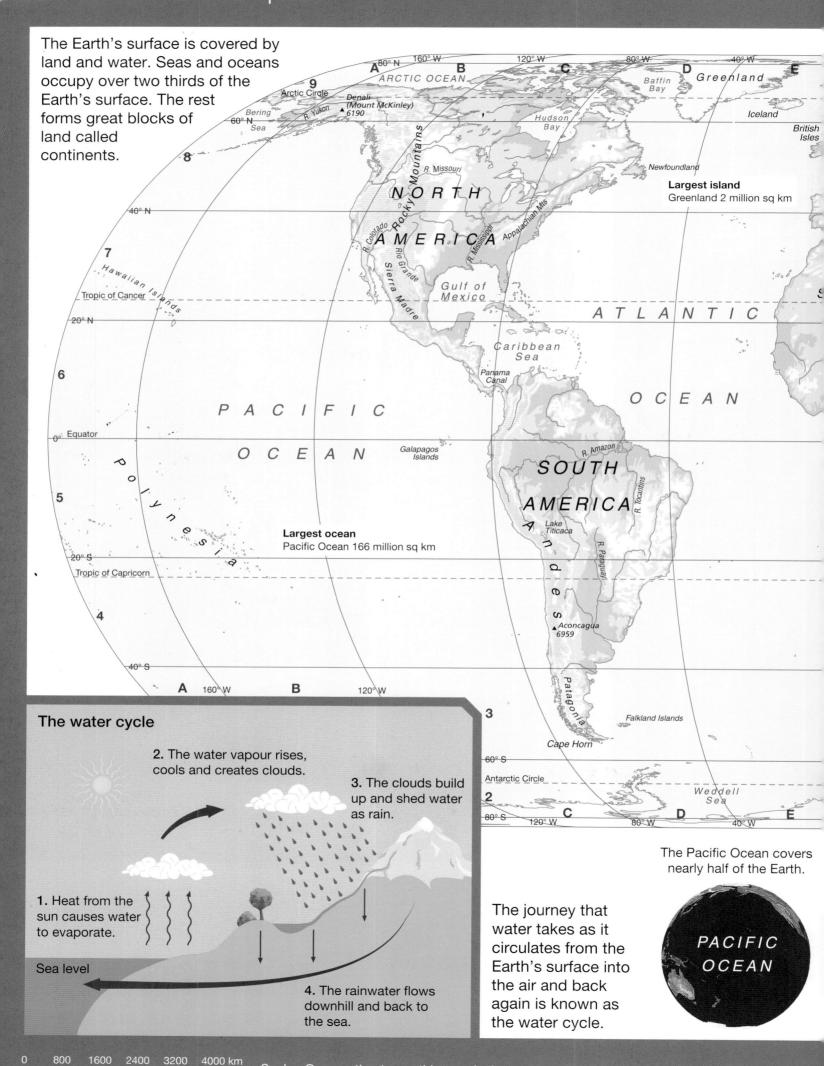

The Earth's surface is covered by land and water. Seas and oceans occupy over two thirds of the Earth's surface. The rest forms great blocks of land called continents.

ARCTIC OCEAN

Arctic Circle

Bering Sea

R. Yukon

Denali (Mount McKinley) ▲ 6190

Rocky Mountains

R. Missouri

NORTH AMERICA

R. Colorado

Rio Grande

Sierra Madre

Appalachian Mts

R. Mississippi

Gulf of Mexico

Hawaiian Islands

Tropic of Cancer

PACIFIC

OCEAN

Polynesia

Equator

Galapagos Islands

Caribbean Sea

Panama Canal

ATLANTIC

OCEAN

SOUTH AMERICA

R. Amazon

Andes

R. Tocantins

Lake Titicaca

R. Paraguay

Tropic of Capricorn

Aconcagua ▲ 6959

Patagonia

Cape Horn

Falkland Islands

Antarctic Circle

Weddell Sea

Baffin Bay

Greenland

Iceland

British Isles

Newfoundland

Hudson Bay

Largest island
Greenland 2 million sq km

Largest ocean
Pacific Ocean 166 million sq km

The water cycle

2. The water vapour rises, cools and creates clouds.

3. The clouds build up and shed water as rain.

1. Heat from the sun causes water to evaporate.

Sea level

4. The rainwater flows downhill and back to the sea.

The Pacific Ocean covers nearly half of the Earth.

The journey that water takes as it circulates from the Earth's surface into the air and back again is known as the water cycle.

PACIFIC OCEAN

0   800   1600   2400   3200   4000 km

Scale : One centimetre on this map is the same as 800 kilometres on the ground.

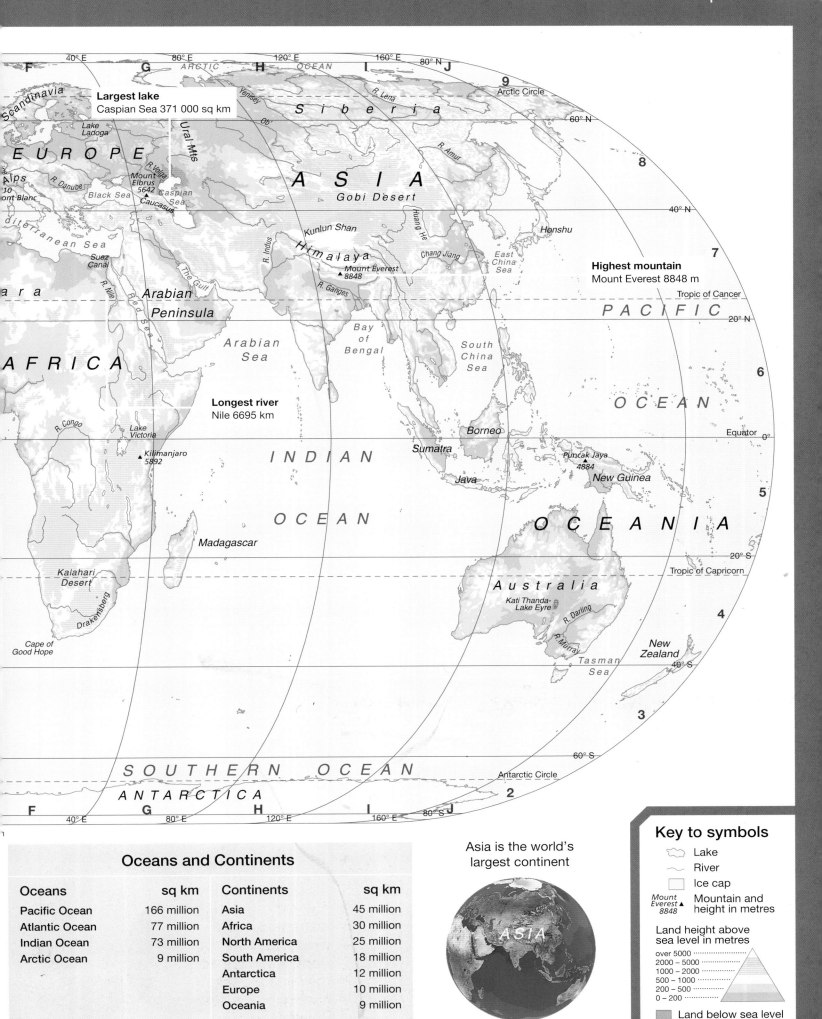

Largest lake
Caspian Sea 371 000 sq km

Highest mountain
Mount Everest 8848 m

Longest river
Nile 6695 km

Map labels:

F G H I J — 40° E, 80° E, 120° E, 160° E, 80° N

Scandinavia
Lake Ladoga
EUROPE
Ural Mts
R. Volga
Mount Elbrus 5642
Alps
Mont Blanc
R. Danube
Black Sea
Caucasus
Caspian Sea
Mediterranean Sea
Suez Canal
R. Nile
Red Sea
The Gulf
ara
AFRICA
R. Congo
Lake Victoria
Kilimanjaro 5892
Kalahari Desert
Drakensberg
Cape of Good Hope
Madagascar

ARCTIC OCEAN
Siberia
Yenisey
Ob
R. Lena
Arctic Circle
60° N
ASIA
R. Amur
Gobi Desert
40° N
Kunlun Shan
R. Indus
Himalaya
Mount Everest 8848
R. Ganges
Huang He
Chang Jiang
Honshu
East China Sea
Tropic of Cancer
Arabian Peninsula
Arabian Sea
Bay of Bengal
South China Sea
20° N
PACIFIC OCEAN
Sumatra
Borneo
Java
New Guinea
Puncak Jaya 4884
Equator 0°
INDIAN OCEAN
OCEANIA
20° S
Australia
Kati Thanda- Lake Eyre
R. Darling
R. Murray
Tropic of Capricorn
New Zealand
Tasman Sea
40° S

9
8
7
6
5
4
3
2

SOUTHERN OCEAN
Antarctic Circle
60° S
ANTARCTICA
F G H I J — 40° E, 80° E, 120° E, 160° E, 80° S

Oceans and Continents

Oceans	sq km	Continents	sq km
Pacific Ocean	166 million	Asia	45 million
Atlantic Ocean	77 million	Africa	30 million
Indian Ocean	73 million	North America	25 million
Arctic Ocean	9 million	South America	18 million
		Antarctica	12 million
		Europe	10 million
		Oceania	9 million

Asia is the world's
largest continent

ASIA

Key to symbols

〰 Lake

⁓ River

▢ Ice cap

Mount Everest▲ 8848   Mountain and height in metres

Land height above sea level in metres

over 5000
2000 – 5000
1000 – 2000
500 – 1000
200 – 500
0 – 200

▨ Land below sea level

The pattern of weather from year to year is called the climate. Places near the Equator have hot climates. Places near the poles have cold climates.

Climate graphs

The red line shows average temperature.
The blue bars show average monthly rainfall.

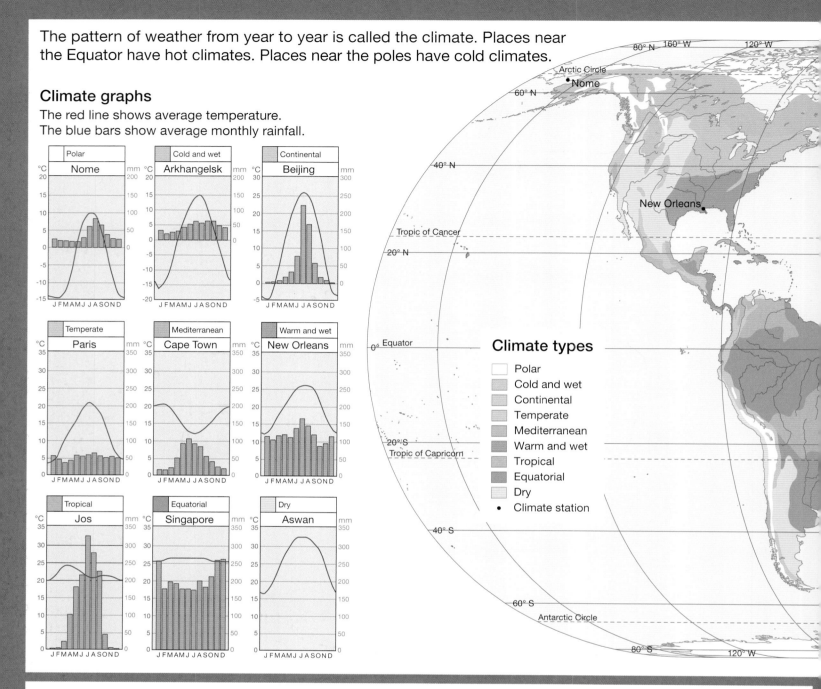

| Polar — Nome | Cold and wet — Arkhangelsk | Continental — Beijing |

| Temperate — Paris | Mediterranean — Cape Town | Warm and wet — New Orleans |

| Tropical — Jos | Equatorial — Singapore | Dry — Aswan |

Climate types

- Polar
- Cold and wet
- Continental
- Temperate
- Mediterranean
- Warm and wet
- Tropical
- Equatorial
- Dry
- • Climate station

Map labels: 80° N, 160° W, 120° W, Arctic Circle, Nome, 60° N, 40° N, New Orleans, Tropic of Cancer, 20° N, Equator 0°, 20° S, Tropic of Capricorn, 40° S, 60° S, Antarctic Circle, 80° S, 120° W

Seasons across the world

The year is divided into seasons. The length of each season can vary depending on how far a place is from the Equator.

These dials show the pattern of seasons in the Northern Hemisphere.

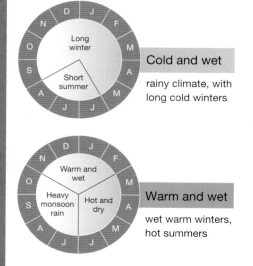

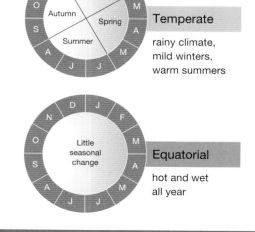

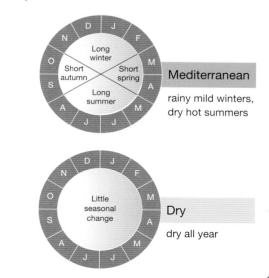

Cold and wet
rainy climate, with long cold winters

Temperate
rainy climate, mild winters, warm summers

Mediterranean
rainy mild winters, dry hot summers

Warm and wet
wet warm winters, hot summers

Equatorial
hot and wet all year

Dry
dry all year

0 1000 2000 3000 4000 5000 km

Scale : One centimetre on this map is the same as 1000 kilometres on the ground.

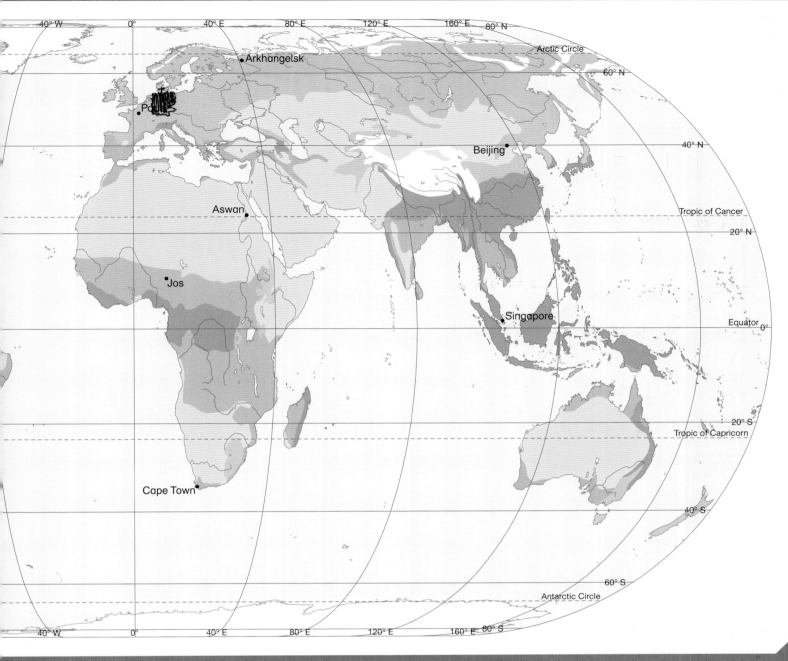

Annual rainfall

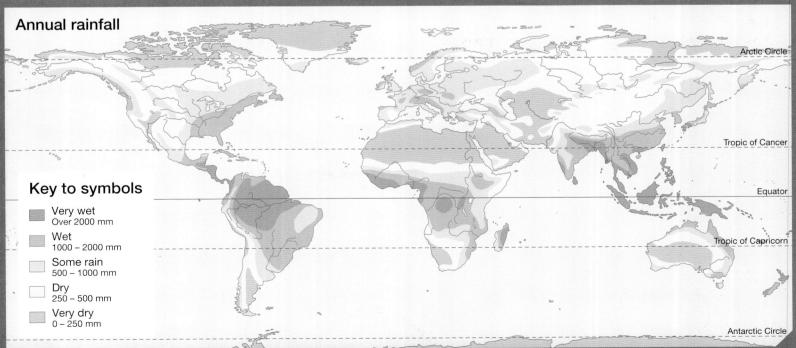

Key to symbols

- Very wet
  Over 2000 mm
- Wet
  1000 – 2000 mm
- Some rain
  500 – 1000 mm
- Dry
  250 – 500 mm
- Very dry
  0 – 250 mm

Roconem

A biome is a large community of plants and animals found in areas of the world with similar soils and climates. There are four main biomes on dry land – forest, grassland, desert and tundra. There are also biomes such as coral reefs in the seas and oceans.

Connell –

Sciatic

• Access – 60 minutes
• Test – General Health
• X-ray

Access – £75
X-ray – £90

Follow
– Report
£47 – Pay as you go –

Jakie – Sat 15th 11:30

Forest
- Coniferous
- Temperate
- Tropical
- Sub tropical
- Monsoon

Grassland
- Savanna
- Temperate

Desert
- Hot desert
- Ice cap and ice shelf

Tundra
- Arctic tundra
- Mountain

★ Coral reefs at risk

More favourable conditions

Very harsh conditions

ARCTIC OCEAN
Arctic Circle
80° N   160° W   120° W   80° W
60° N
40° N
Tropic of Cancer
20° N
Equator   0°
20° S
Tropic of Capricorn
40° S
60° S
Antarctic Circle
80° S   160° W   120° W   80° W   40

ATLANTIC OCEAN
PACIFIC OCEAN

Wild boar
Siberian tiger
Red squirrel

22nd – 10am

Wildebeest
Lion
Giraffe

Forests cover about a third of the land. The type of forest changes with the latitude.

Grasslands are used as grazing areas by animals and as farming grounds by humans.

0   900   1800   2700   3600   4500 km

Scale : One centimetre on this map is the same as 900 kilometres on the ground.

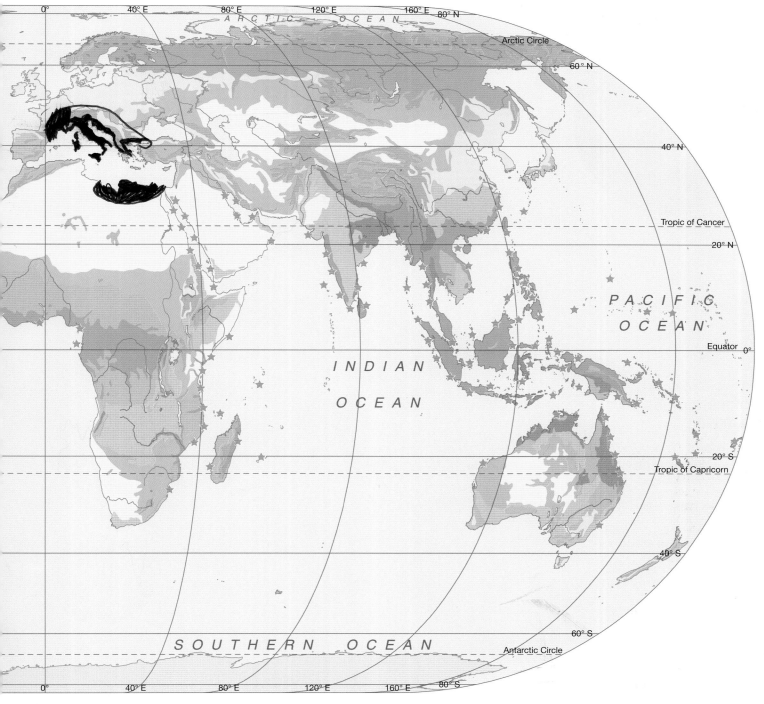

Meerkat

Camel

Springbok

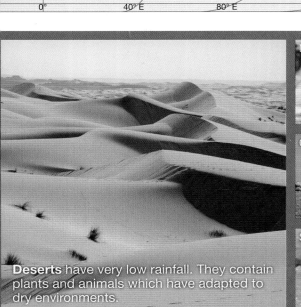

Deserts have very low rainfall. They contain plants and animals which have adapted to dry environments.

Tundra is a very cold biome but supports a surprising number of shrubs, lichens, mosses and flowers.

Arctic poppy

Polar bear

Snow geese

Inside the Earth

Crust
Mantle
Outer core
Inner core

Major volcanic eruptions 1980–2016

Year	Location
1980	Mount St Helens, USA
1982	El Chichónal, Mexico
1982	Gunung Galunggung, Indonesia
1983	Kilauea, Hawaii, USA
1983	O-yama, Japan
1985	Nevado del Ruiz, Colombia
1991	Mount Pinatubo, Philippines
1991	Unzen-dake, Japan
1993	Mayon, Philippines
1993	Volcán Galeras, Colombia
1994	Volcán Llaima, Chile
1994	Rabaul, Papua New Guinea
1997	Soufrière Hills, Montserrat
2000	Hekla, Iceland
2001	Mount Etna, Italy
2002	Nyiragongo, Dem. Rep. of the Congo
2010	Eyjafjallajökull, Iceland
2010	Mount Merapi, Indonesia
2014	Mount Ontake, Japan

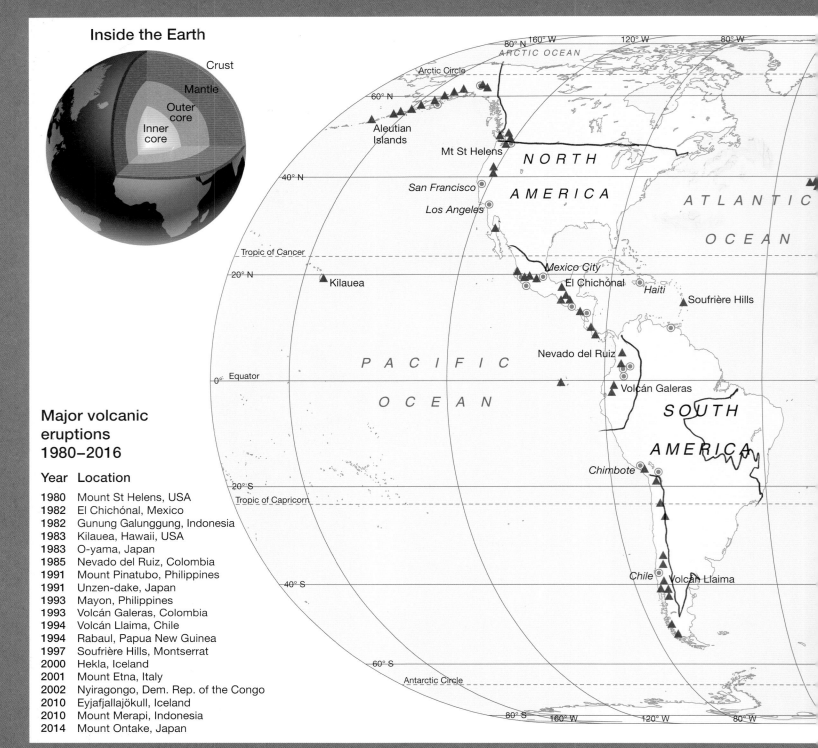

Arctic Circle
ARCTIC OCEAN
NORTH AMERICA
ATLANTIC OCEAN
Aleutian Islands
Mt St Helens
San Francisco
Los Angeles
Tropic of Cancer
Kilauea
Mexico City
El Chichónal
Haiti
Soufrière Hills
Nevado del Ruiz
PACIFIC OCEAN
Volcán Galeras
SOUTH AMERICA
Equator
Chimbote
Tropic of Capricorn
Chile
Volcán Llaima
Antarctic Circle

In 2010, a volcano in Iceland erupted sending a huge cloud of ash 10 000 metres into the sky. Wind blew the ash hundreds of kilometres south over Western Europe. The ash cloud caused serious disruptions to air travel.

Pacific Ring of Fire

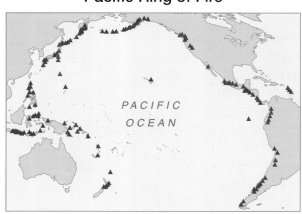

PACIFIC OCEAN

The 'Pacific Ring of Fire' is an area around the Pacific Ocean where there are many active volcanoes and earthquakes.

0   900   1800   2700   3600   4500 km

Scale : One centimetre on this map is the same as 900 kilometres on the ground.

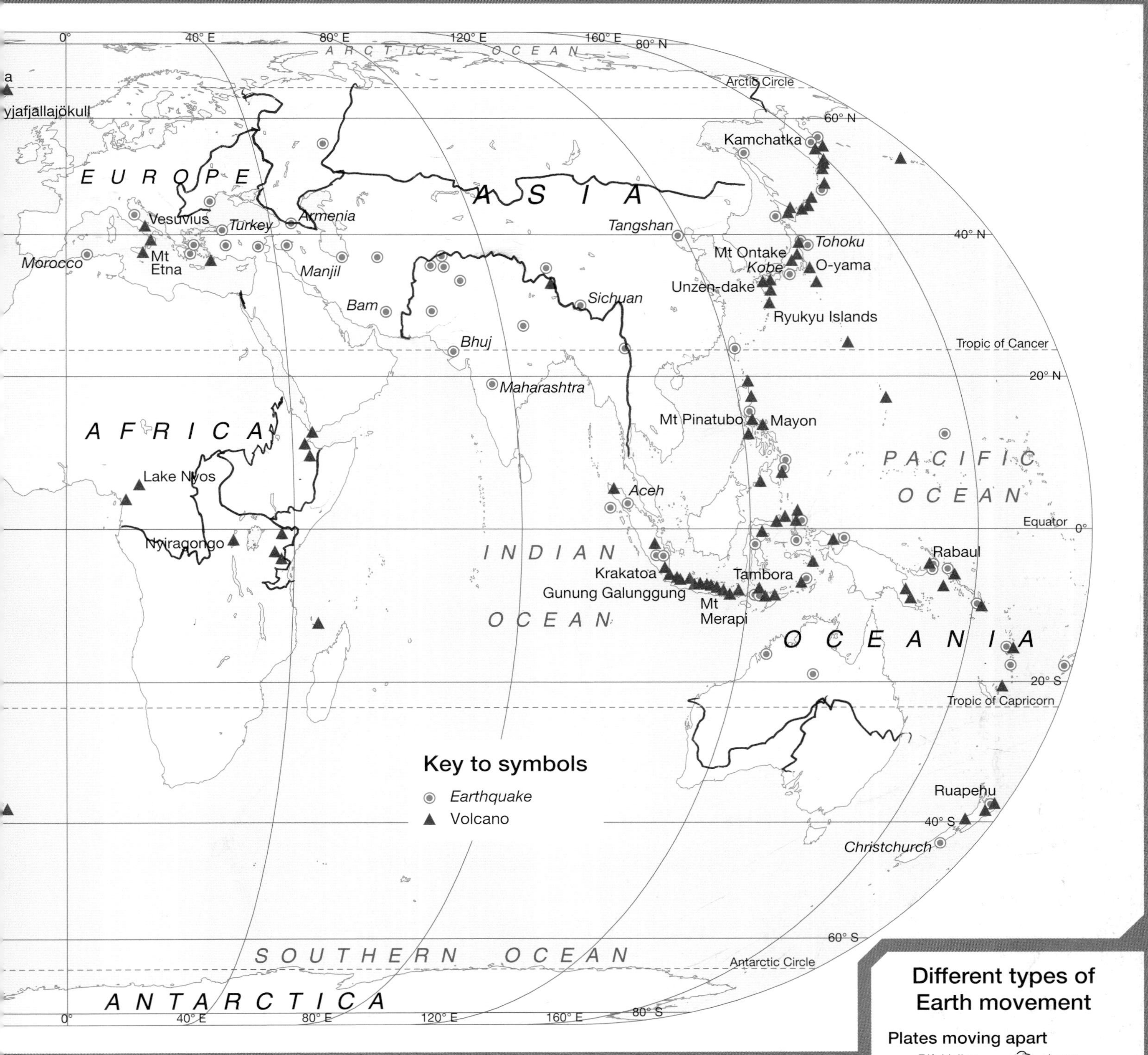
0°
40° E
80° E
120° E
160° E
80° N
ARCTIC OCEAN
Arctic Circle
60° N
yjafjallajökull
EUROPE
ASIA
Kamchatka
Vesuvius
Turkey
Armenia
Tangshan
Morocco
Mt Etna
Manjil
Mt Ontake
Tohoku
Kobe
O-yama
40° N
Unzen-dake
Bam
Sichuan
Ryukyu Islands
Bhuj
Tropic of Cancer
20° N
Maharashtra
AFRICA
Mt Pinatubo
Mayon
PACIFIC OCEAN
Lake Nyos
Aceh
Equator
0°
Nyiragongo
INDIAN OCEAN
Rabaul
Krakatoa
Tambora
Gunung Galunggung
Mt Merapi
OCEANIA
20° S
Tropic of Capricorn
Key to symbols
Earthquake
Volcano
Ruapehu
40° S
Christchurch
60° S
SOUTHERN OCEAN
Antarctic Circle
ANTARCTICA
80° S

The movement of the hot rocks which lie deep inside the Earth is sometimes felt on the surface. When hot rocks and gas erupt through an opening it creates a volcano. In other places sudden shifts in the Earth's crust causes earthquakes. If these movements happen near or under the sea they can result in huge waves known as a tsunami.

Plate boundaries

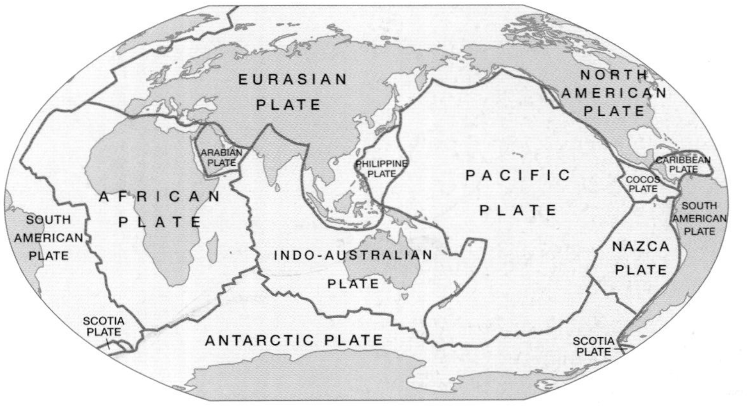
EURASIAN PLATE
NORTH AMERICAN PLATE
ARABIAN PLATE
PHILIPPINE PLATE
CARIBBEAN PLATE
PACIFIC PLATE
COCOS PLATE
AFRICAN PLATE
SOUTH AMERICAN PLATE
SOUTH AMERICAN PLATE
INDO-AUSTRALIAN PLATE
NAZCA PLATE
SCOTIA PLATE
ANTARCTIC PLATE
SCOTIA PLATE

The Earth's crust is broken into great blocks called plates. These move very slowly in different directions.

Different types of Earth movement

Plates moving apart

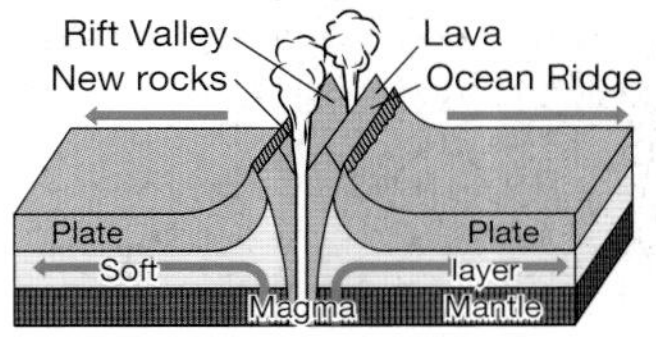
Rift Valley
New rocks
Lava
Ocean Ridge
Plate
Plate
Soft
layer
Magma
Mantle

Plates moving together

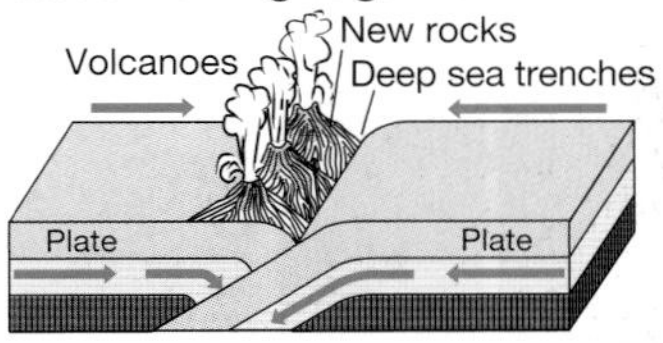
Volcanoes
New rocks
Deep sea trenches
Plate
Plate

Plates moving past each other

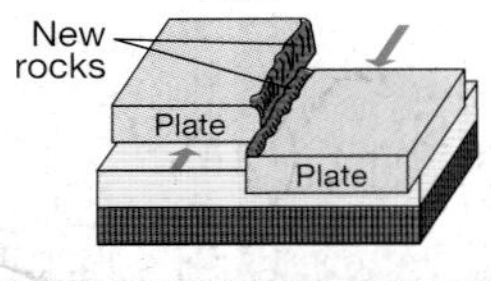
New rocks
Plate
Plate

There are over seven billion people in the world today. Numbers are expected to go on rising till at least 2050 by which time there will be nine billion people or more.

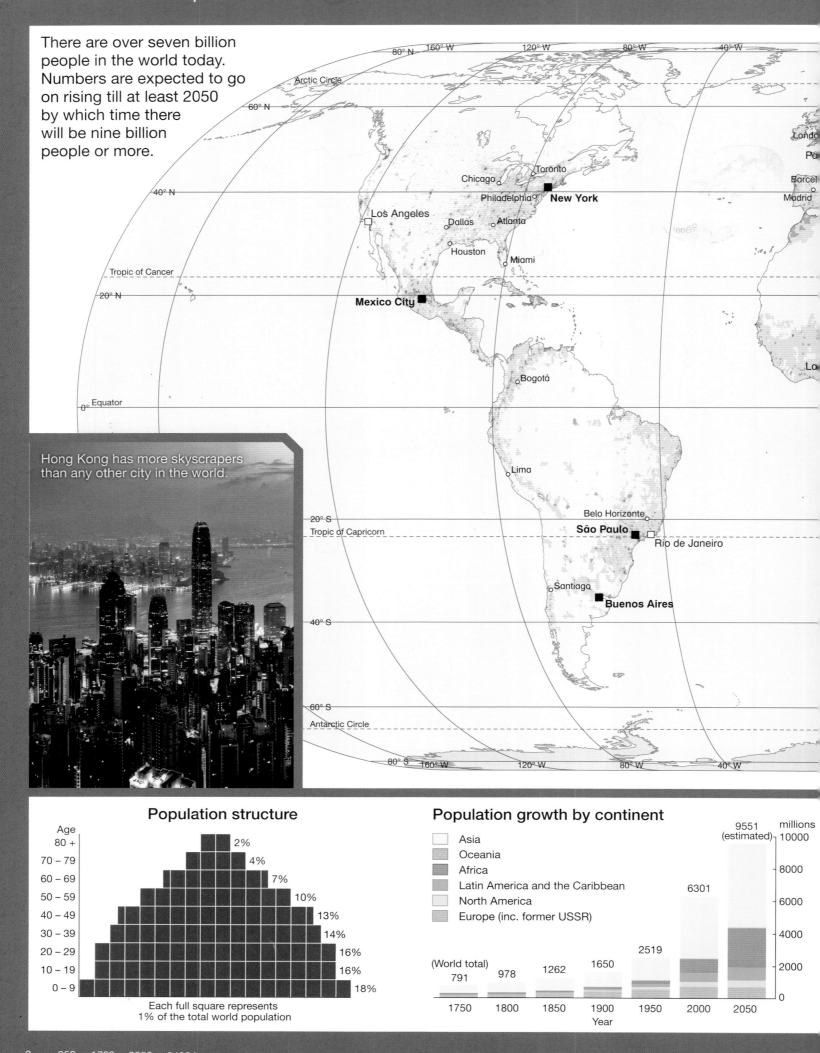

Hong Kong has more skyscrapers than any other city in the world.

Map labels:
80° N, 160° W, 120° W, 80° W, 40° W
Arctic Circle
60° N
London
Po
Barcel
40° N
Madrid
Toronto
Chicago
Philadelphia
New York
Los Angeles
Dallas
Atlanta
Houston
Miami
Tropic of Cancer
20° N
Mexico City
La
Bogotá
0° Equator
Lima
Belo Horizonte
20° S   Tropic of Capricorn
São Paulo
Rio de Janeiro
Santiago
Buenos Aires
40° S
60° S
Antarctic Circle
80° S   160° W   120° W   80° W   40° W

Population structure

Age	
80 +	2%
70 – 79	4%
60 – 69	7%
50 – 59	10%
40 – 49	13%
30 – 39	14%
20 – 29	16%
10 – 19	16%
0 – 9	18%

Each full square represents 1% of the total world population

Population growth by continent

- Asia
- Oceania
- Africa
- Latin America and the Caribbean
- North America
- Europe (inc. former USSR)

millions
10000
9551 (estimated)
8000
6301
6000
4000
2519
2000
(World total)
791   978   1262   1650
0

1750   1800   1850   1900   1950   2000   2050
Year

0   850   1700   2550   3400 km

Scale : One centimetre on this map is the same as 850 kilometres on the ground.

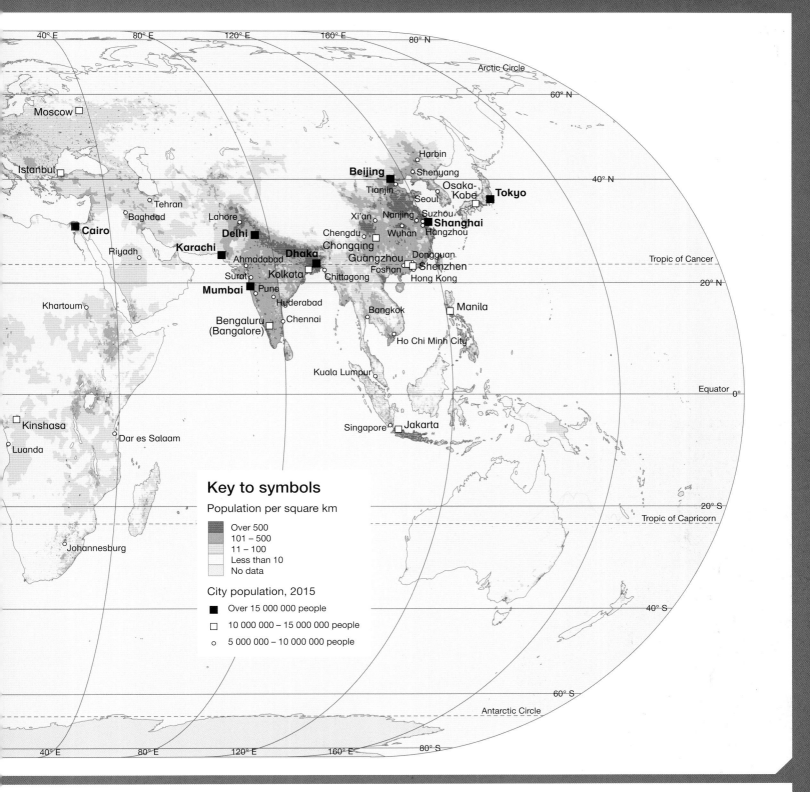

Key to symbols

Population per square km

- Over 500
- 101 – 500
- 11 – 100
- Less than 10
- No data

City population, 2015

- ■ Over 15 000 000 people
- □ 10 000 000 – 15 000 000 people
- ○ 5 000 000 – 10 000 000 people

Largest cities

Millions (0–40)

Dhaka, New York, Cairo, Beijing, Mexico City, Mumbai, São Paulo, Shanghai, Delhi, Tokyo

Global village

If the world were a community of 100 people this is what it would be like.

- **8** from Europe
- **2** from Russia
- **8** from North America
- **60** from Asia
- **6** from South America
- **15** from Africa
- **1** from Oceania

Throughout history people have moved home to live in other countries. Some are driven out by war, others go in search of a better life.

Key to symbols

Origin of migrants

→ European Jew
→ African (slaves)
→ Caribbean
→ European
→ Mexican

→ Indian/Pakistani
→ Southeast Asian
→ Chinese
→ Japanese

World migration since 1600

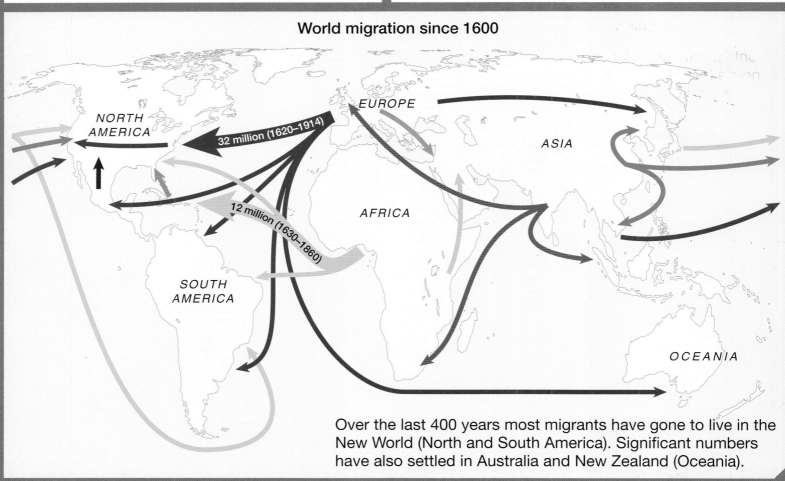

32 million (1620–1914)

12 million (1630–1860)

NORTH AMERICA

EUROPE

ASIA

AFRICA

SOUTH AMERICA

OCEANIA

Over the last 400 years most migrants have gone to live in the New World (North and South America). Significant numbers have also settled in Australia and New Zealand (Oceania).

Refugees

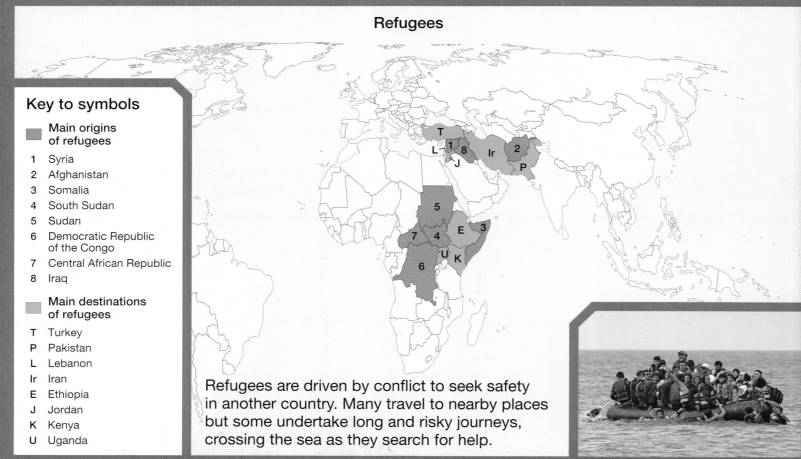

Key to symbols

Main origins of refugees

1 Syria
2 Afghanistan
3 Somalia
4 South Sudan
5 Sudan
6 Democratic Republic of the Congo
7 Central African Republic
8 Iraq

Main destinations of refugees

T Turkey
P Pakistan
L Lebanon
Ir Iran
E Ethiopia
J Jordan
K Kenya
U Uganda

Refugees are driven by conflict to seek safety in another country. Many travel to nearby places but some undertake long and risky journeys, crossing the sea as they search for help.

| 0 | 1400 | 2800 | 4200 | 5600 | 7000 km |

Scale : One centimetre on this map is the same as 1400 kilometres on the ground.

People have always traded goods with each other but today we depend more than ever on our links with other countries. This is known as globalisation.

World farming, mining and shipping

Countries with good farmland and plenty of minerals trade their products around the world. Shipping routes link major cities. Oil, coal and wheat are important cargoes.

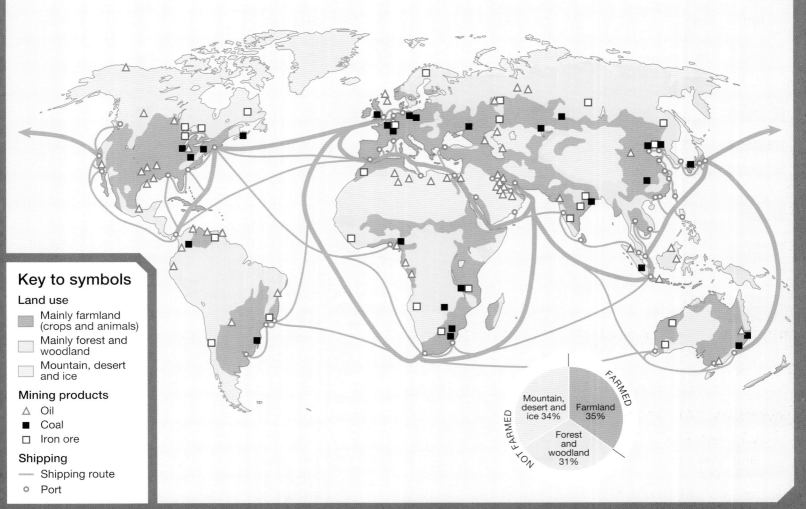

Key to symbols

Land use

- Mainly farmland (crops and animals)
- Mainly forest and woodland
- Mountain, desert and ice

Mining products

- △ Oil
- ■ Coal
- □ Iron ore

Shipping

- — Shipping route
- ○ Port

Mountain, desert and ice 34%

Farmland 35%

Forest and woodland 31%

FARMED

NOT FARMED

Exports are goods which are sent from one country to another.

Banana exporters	Wheat exporters	Car exporters	Toy exporters	Oil exporters
1. Ecuador	1. USA	1. Germany	1. China	1. Saudi Arabia
2. Philippines	2. France	2. Japan	2. USA	2. Russia
3. Costa Rica	3. Australia	3. USA	3. Netherlands	3. Iraq
4. Colombia	4. Canada	4. Canada	4. Germany	4. United Arab Emirates
5. Guatemala	5. Russia	5. South Korea	5. Czechia (Czech Republic)	5. Canada

| 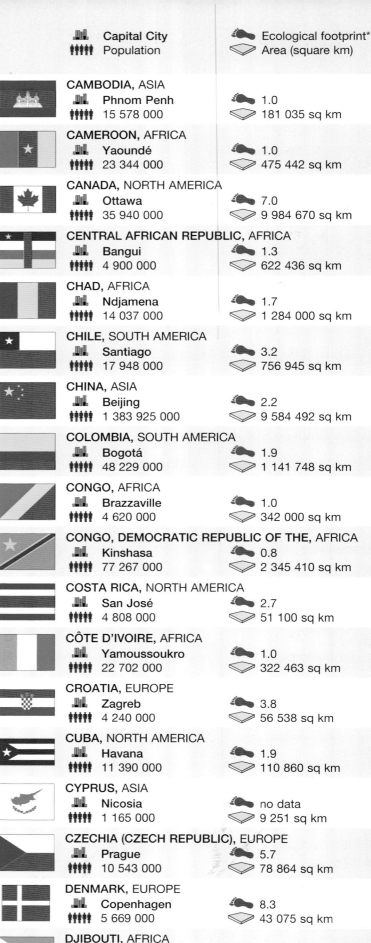 Capital City |
| Population |

| Ecological footprint* |
| Area (square km) |

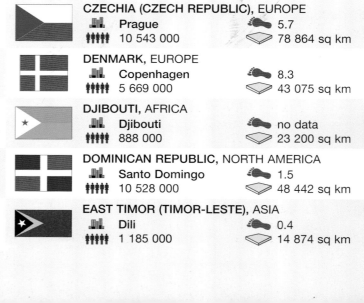

AFGHANISTAN, ASIA
Kabul 0.6
32 527 000 652 225 sq km

ALBANIA, EUROPE
Tirana 1.9
2 897 000 28 748 sq km

ALGERIA, AFRICA
Algiers 1.6
39 667 000 2 381 741 sq km

ANGOLA, AFRICA
Luanda 1.0
25 022 000 1 246 700 sq km

ARGENTINA, SOUTH AMERICA
Buenos Aires 2.6
43 417 000 2 766 889 sq km

ARMENIA, ASIA
Yerevan 1.8
3 018 000 29 800 sq km

AUSTRALIA, OCEANIA
Canberra 6.8
23 969 000 7 692 024 sq km

AUSTRIA, EUROPE
Vienna 5.3
8 545 000 83 855 sq km

AZERBAIJAN, ASIA
Baku 1.9
9 754 000 86 600 sq km

BANGLADESH, ASIA
Dhaka 0.6
160 996 000 143 998 sq km

BELARUS, EUROPE
Minsk 3.8
9 496 000 207 600 sq km

BELGIUM, EUROPE
Brussels 8.0
11 299 000 30 520 sq km

BENIN, AFRICA
Porto-Novo 1.2
10 880 000 112 620 sq km

BOLIVIA, SOUTH AMERICA
La Paz/Sucre 2.6
10 725 000 1 098 581 sq km

BOSNIA AND HERZEGOVINA, EUROPE
Sarajevo 2.8
3 810 000 51 130 sq km

BOTSWANA, AFRICA
Gaborone 2.7
2 262 000 581 370 sq km

BRAZIL, SOUTH AMERICA
Brasília 2.9
207 848 000 8 514 879 sq km

BULGARIA, EUROPE
Sofia 4.1
7 150 000 110 994 sq km

BURKINA FASO, AFRICA
Ouagadougou 1.3
18 106 000 274 200 sq km

BURUNDI, AFRICA
Bujumbura 0.9
11 179 000 27 835 sq km

CAMBODIA, ASIA
Phnom Penh 1.0
15 578 000 181 035 sq km

CAMEROON, AFRICA
Yaoundé 1.0
23 344 000 475 442 sq km

CANADA, NORTH AMERICA
Ottawa 7.0
35 940 000 9 984 670 sq km

CENTRAL AFRICAN REPUBLIC, AFRICA
Bangui 1.3
4 900 000 622 436 sq km

CHAD, AFRICA
Ndjamena 1.7
14 037 000 1 284 000 sq km

CHILE, SOUTH AMERICA
Santiago 3.2
17 948 000 756 945 sq km

CHINA, ASIA
Beijing 2.2
1 383 925 000 9 584 492 sq km

COLOMBIA, SOUTH AMERICA
Bogotá 1.9
48 229 000 1 141 748 sq km

CONGO, AFRICA
Brazzaville 1.0
4 620 000 342 000 sq km

CONGO, DEMOCRATIC REPUBLIC OF THE, AFRICA
Kinshasa 0.8
77 267 000 2 345 410 sq km

COSTA RICA, NORTH AMERICA
San José 2.7
4 808 000 51 100 sq km

CÔTE D'IVOIRE, AFRICA
Yamoussoukro 1.0
22 702 000 322 463 sq km

CROATIA, EUROPE
Zagreb 3.8
4 240 000 56 538 sq km

CUBA, NORTH AMERICA
Havana 1.9
11 390 000 110 860 sq km

CYPRUS, ASIA
Nicosia no data
1 165 000 9 251 sq km

CZECHIA (CZECH REPUBLIC), EUROPE
Prague 5.7
10 543 000 78 864 sq km

DENMARK, EUROPE
Copenhagen 8.3
5 669 000 43 075 sq km

DJIBOUTI, AFRICA
Djibouti no data
888 000 23 200 sq km

DOMINICAN REPUBLIC, NORTH AMERICA
Santo Domingo 1.5
10 528 000 48 442 sq km

EAST TIMOR (TIMOR-LESTE), ASIA
Dili 0.4
1 185 000 14 874 sq km

*Ecological footprints measure the average amount of land (hectares) each person needs to support their way of living. High figures indicate high consumption. Low figures indicate greater sustainability. The world average is 2.7.

ECUADOR, SOUTH AMERICA
Quito — 1.9
16 144 000 — 272 045 sq km

EGYPT, AFRICA
Cairo — 1.7
91 508 000 — 1 001 450 sq km

EL SALVADOR, NORTH AMERICA
San Salvador — 2.0
6 127 000 — 21 041 sq km

ERITREA, AFRICA
Asmara — 0.9
5 228 000 — 117 400 sq km

ESTONIA, EUROPE
Tallinn — 7.9
1 313 000 — 45 200 sq km

ETHIOPIA, AFRICA
Addis Ababa — 1.1
99 391 000 — 1 133 880 sq km

FINLAND, EUROPE
Helsinki — 6.2
5 503 000 — 338 145 sq km

FRANCE, EUROPE
Paris — 5.0
64 395 000 — 543 965 sq km

GABON, AFRICA
Libreville — 1.4
1 725 000 — 267 667 sq km

GEORGIA, ASIA
Tbilisi — 1.8
4 000 000 — 69 700 sq km

GERMANY, EUROPE
Berlin — 5.1
80 689 000 — 357 022 sq km

GHANA, AFRICA
Accra — 1.8
27 410 000 — 238 537 sq km

GREECE, EUROPE
Athens — 5.4
10 955 000 — 131 957 sq km

GUATEMALA, NORTH AMERICA
Guatemala City — 1.8
16 343 000 — 108 890 sq km

GUINEA, AFRICA
Conakry — 1.7
12 609 000 — 245 857 sq km

GUINEA-BISSAU, AFRICA
Bissau — 1.0
1 844 000 — 36 125 sq km

GUYANA, SOUTH AMERICA
Georgetown — 2.4
767 000 — 214 969 sq km

HAITI, NORTH AMERICA
Port-au-Prince — 0.7
10 711 000 — 27 750 sq km

HONDURAS, NORTH AMERICA
Tegucigalpa — 1.9
8 075 000 — 112 088 sq km

HUNGARY, EUROPE
Budapest — 3.0
9 855 000 — 93 030 sq km

ICELAND, EUROPE
Reykjavík — 6.5
329 000 — 102 820 sq km

INDIA, ASIA
New Delhi — 0.9
1 311 051 000 — 3 064 898 sq km

INDONESIA, ASIA
Jakarta — 1.2
257 564 000 — 1 919 445 sq km

IRAN, ASIA
Tehran — 2.7
79 109 000 — 1 648 000 sq km

IRAQ, ASIA
Baghdad — 1.4
36 423 000 — 438 317 sq km

IRELAND, EUROPE
Dublin — 6.3
4 688 000 — 70 282 sq km

ISRAEL, ASIA
Jerusalem† — 4.8
8 064 000 — 22 072 sq km

ITALY, EUROPE
Rome — 5.0
59 798 000 — 301 245 sq km

JAMAICA, NORTH AMERICA
Kingston — 1.9
2 793 000 — 10 991 sq km

JAPAN, ASIA
Tokyo — 4.7
126 573 000 — 377 727 sq km

JORDAN, ASIA
Amman — 2.1
7 595 000 — 89 206 sq km

KAZAKHSTAN, ASIA
Astana — 4.5
17 625 000 — 2 717 300 sq km

KENYA, AFRICA
Nairobi — 1.1
46 050 000 — 582 646 sq km

KOSOVO, EUROPE
Pristina — no data
1 805 000 — 10 908 sq km

KUWAIT, ASIA
Kuwait — 6.3
3 892 000 — 17 818 sq km

KYRGYZSTAN, ASIA
Bishkek — 1.3
5 940 000 — 198 500 sq km

LAOS, ASIA
Vientiane — 1.3
6 802 000 — 236 800 sq km

LATVIA, EUROPE
Riga — 5.6
1 971 000 — 64 589 sq km

LEBANON, ASIA
Beirut — 2.9
5 851 000 — 10 452 sq km

LESOTHO, AFRICA
Maseru — 1.1
2 135 000 — 30 355 sq km

† Disputed capital

🏙 Capital City   👣 Ecological footprint*
👫 Population   ◇ Area (square km)

LIBERIA, AFRICA
🏙 Monrovia   👣 1.3
👫 4 503 000   ◇ 111 369 sq km

LIBYA, AFRICA
🏙 Tripoli   👣 3.1
👫 6 278 000   ◇ 1 759 540 sq km

LITHUANIA, EUROPE
🏙 Vilnius   👣 4.7
👫 2 878 000   ◇ 65 200 sq km

LUXEMBOURG, EUROPE
🏙 Luxembourg   👣 no data
👫 567 000   ◇ 2 586 sq km

MACEDONIA (F.Y.R.O.M.), EUROPE
🏙 Skopje   👣 5.7
👫 2 078 000   ◇ 25 713 sq km

MADAGASCAR, AFRICA
🏙 Antananarivo   👣 1.8
👫 24 235 000   ◇ 587 041 sq km

MALAWI, AFRICA
🏙 Lilongwe   👣 0.7
👫 17 215 000   ◇ 118 484 sq km

MALAYSIA, ASIA
🏙 Kuala Lumpur/Putrajaya   👣 4.9
👫 30 331 000   ◇ 332 965 sq km

MALI, AFRICA
🏙 Bamako   👣 1.9
👫 17 600 000   ◇ 1 240 140 sq km

MAURITANIA, AFRICA
🏙 Nouakchott   👣 2.6
👫 4 068 000   ◇ 1 030 700 sq km

MEXICO, NORTH AMERICA
🏙 Mexico City   👣 3.0
👫 127 017 000   ◇ 1 972 545 sq km

MOLDOVA, EUROPE
🏙 Chişinău   👣 1.4
👫 4 069 000   ◇ 33 700 sq km

MONGOLIA, ASIA
🏙 Ulan Bator   👣 5.5
👫 2 959 000   ◇ 1 565 000 sq km

MONTENEGRO, EUROPE
🏙 Podgorica   👣 no data
👫 626 000   ◇ 13 812 sq km

MOROCCO, AFRICA
🏙 Rabat   👣 1.2
👫 34 378 000   ◇ 446 550 sq km

MOZAMBIQUE, AFRICA
🏙 Maputo   👣 0.8
👫 27 978 000   ◇ 799 380 sq km

MYANMAR (BURMA), ASIA
🏙 Nay Pyi Taw   👣 1.8
👫 53 897 000   ◇ 676 577 sq km

NAMIBIA, AFRICA
🏙 Windhoek   👣 2.2
👫 2 459 000   ◇ 824 292 sq km

NEPAL, ASIA
🏙 Kathmandu   👣 3.6
👫 28 514 000   ◇ 147 181 sq km

NETHERLANDS, EUROPE
🏙 Amsterdam/The Hague   👣 6.2
👫 16 925 000   ◇ 41 526 sq km

NEW ZEALAND, OCEANIA
🏙 Wellington   👣 4.9
👫 4 529 000   ◇ 270 534 sq km

NICARAGUA, NORTH AMERICA
🏙 Managua   👣 1.6
👫 6 082 000   ◇ 130 000 sq km

NIGER, AFRICA
🏙 Niamey   👣 2.4
👫 19 899 000   ◇ 1 267 000 sq km

NIGERIA, AFRICA
🏙 Abuja   👣 1.4
👫 182 202 000   ◇ 923 768 sq km

NORTH KOREA, ASIA
🏙 Pyongyang   👣 1.3
👫 25 155 000   ◇ 120 538 sq km

NORWAY, EUROPE
🏙 Oslo   👣 5.6
👫 5 211 000   ◇ 323 878 sq km

OMAN, ASIA
🏙 Muscat   👣 5.0
👫 4 491 000   ◇ 309 500 sq km

PAKISTAN, ASIA
🏙 Islamabad   👣 0.8
👫 188 925 000   ◇ 803 940 sq km

PANAMA, NORTH AMERICA
🏙 Panama City   👣 2.9
👫 3 929 000   ◇ 77 082 sq km

PAPUA NEW GUINEA, OCEANIA
🏙 Port Moresby   👣 2.1
👫 7 619 000   ◇ 462 840 sq km

PARAGUAY, SOUTH AMERICA
🏙 Asunción   👣 3.2
👫 6 639 000   ◇ 406 752 sq km

PERU, SOUTH AMERICA
🏙 Lima   👣 1.5
👫 31 377 000   ◇ 1 285 216 sq km

PHILIPPINES, ASIA
🏙 Manila   👣 1.3
👫 100 699 000   ◇ 300 000 sq km

POLAND, EUROPE
🏙 Warsaw   👣 4.4
👫 38 612 000   ◇ 312 683 sq km

PORTUGAL, EUROPE
🏙 Lisbon   👣 4.5
👫 10 350 000   ◇ 88 940 sq km

QATAR, ASIA
🏙 Doha   👣 10.5
👫 2 235 000   ◇ 11 437 sq km

ROMANIA, EUROPE
🏙 Bucharest   👣 2.7
👫 19 511 000   ◇ 237 500 sq km

RUSSIA, EUROPE/ASIA
🏙 Moscow   👣 4.4
👫 143 457 000   ◇ 17 075 400 sq km

RWANDA, AFRICA
🏙 Kigali   👣 1.0
👫 11 610 000   ◇ 26 338 sq km

SAUDI ARABIA, ASIA
🏙 Riyadh   👣 5.1
👫 31 540 000   ◇ 2 200 000 sq km

*Ecological footprints measure the average amount of land (hectares) each person needs to support their way of living. High figures indicate high consumption. Low figures indicate greater sustainability. The world average is 2.7.

World Flags and key data 75

SENEGAL, AFRICA
Dakar
15 129 000
1.1
196 720 sq km

SERBIA, EUROPE
Belgrade
7 046 000
2.4
77 453 sq km

SIERRA LEONE, AFRICA
Freetown
6 453 000
1.1
71 740 sq km

SINGAPORE, ASIA
Singapore
5 604 000
5.3
639 sq km

SLOVAKIA, EUROPE
Bratislava
5 426 000
4.1
49 035 sq km

SLOVENIA, EUROPE
Ljubljana
2 068 000
5.3
20 251 sq km

SOMALIA, AFRICA
Mogadishu
10 787 000
1.4
637 657 sq km

SOUTH AFRICA, AFRICA
Bloemfontein/Pretoria/Cape Town
54 490 000
2.3
1 219 090 sq km

SOUTH KOREA, ASIA
Seoul
50 293 000
4.9
99 274 sq km

SOUTH SUDAN, AFRICA
Juba
12 340 000
no data
644 329 sq km

SPAIN, EUROPE
Madrid
46 122 000
5.4
504 782 sq km

SRI LANKA, ASIA
Sri Jayewardenepura Kotte
20 715 000
1.2
65 610 sq km

SUDAN, AFRICA
Khartoum
40 235 000
no data
1 861 484 sq km

SURINAME, SOUTH AMERICA
Paramaribo
543 000
no data
163 820 sq km

SWAZILAND, AFRICA
Mbabane
1 287 000
1.5
17 364 sq km

SWEDEN, EUROPE
Stockholm
9 779 000
5.9
449 964 sq km

SWITZERLAND, EUROPE
Bern
8 299 000
5.0
41 293 sq km

SYRIA, ASIA
Damascus
18 502 000
1.5
184 026 sq km

TAIWAN, ASIA
Taipei
23 462 000
no data
36 179 sq km

TAJIKISTAN, ASIA
Dushanbe
8 482 000
1.0
143 100 sq km

TANZANIA, AFRICA
Dodoma
53 470 000
1.2
945 087 sq km

THAILAND, ASIA
Bangkok
67 959 000
2.4
513 115 sq km

THE GAMBIA, AFRICA
Banjul
1 991 000
3.5
11 295 sq km

TOGO, AFRICA
Lomé
7 305 000
1.0
56 785 sq km

TRINIDAD AND TOBAGO, SOUTH AMERICA
Port of Spain
1 360 000
3.1
5 130 sq km

TUNISIA, AFRICA
Tunis
11 254 000
1.9
164 150 sq km

TURKEY, ASIA
Ankara
78 666 000
2.7
779 452 sq km

TURKMENISTAN, ASIA
Ashgabat
5 374 000
3.9
488 100 sq km

UGANDA, AFRICA
Kampala
39 032 000
1.5
241 038 sq km

UKRAINE, EUROPE
Kiev
44 824 000
2.9
603 700 sq km

UNITED ARAB EMIRATES, ASIA
Abu Dhabi
9 157 000
10.7
77 700 sq km

UNITED KINGDOM, EUROPE
London
64 716 000
4.9
243 609 sq km

UNITED STATES OF AMERICA, NORTH AMERICA
Washington D.C.
321 774 000
8.0
9 826 635 sq km

URUGUAY, SOUTH AMERICA
Montevideo
3 432 000
5.1
176 215 sq km

UZBEKISTAN, ASIA
Tashkent
29 893 000
1.7
447 400 sq km

VENEZUELA, SOUTH AMERICA
Caracas
31 108 000
2.9
912 050 sq km

VIETNAM, ASIA
Hanoi
93 448 000
1.4
329 565 sq km

YEMEN, ASIA
Sanaa
26 832 000
0.9
527 968 sq km

ZAMBIA, AFRICA
Lusaka
16 212 000
0.9
752 614 sq km

ZIMBABWE, AFRICA
Harare
15 603 000
1.3
390 759 sq km

place name | grid code
Nairobi *capital* 37 C3
page number
cities and towns are shown in green

place name | grid code
Severn *river* 18 E3
page number
water features are shown in blue

place name | grid code
Switzerland *country* 32 F4
page number
countries and states are shown in red

place name | grid code
Borneo *island* 43 D3
page number
physical features are shown in black